O Come, Let God Adore Us

Other Works by Al Hill

Our Evil—God's Good
And Other Sermons from Genesis through Joshua

Things That Kings Can't Do
And Other Sermons from Judges through 2nd Kings, and the Wisdom Books

In the Presence of the Lord
And Other Sermons from the Psalms and the Prophets

Walking with Jesus
And Other Sermons from the Gospel of Matthew

God's Purpose for Your Faith
And Other Sermons from the Gospel of Mark, Hebrews, James and 1st Peter

From Jerusalem to Jericho
And Other Sermons from the Gospel of Luke and the Acts of the Apostles

Traits of the Shepherd
And Other Sermons from the Gospel of John, 1st John and Revelation

Making Peace with Your Father
And Other Sermons from Paul's Letters to the Romans and Corinthians

The Empty God
And Other Sermons from the Shorter Letters of Paul

Not Exactly What They Expected
And Other Sermons for Holy Week and Easter

DEAR TRINITY
Letters from a Pastor to His People

O Come, Let God Adore Us

And Other Sermons for Advent and Christmas

Al Hill

SOMMERTON
HOUSE

Copyright © 2018 Al Hill

All rights reserved. No part of this book may be used or reproduced by any means, graphic, electronic, or mechanical, including photocopying, recording, taping or by any information storage retrieval system without the written permission of the author except in the case of brief quotations embedded in critical articles and reviews.

Scripture quotations marked "KJV" are from the King James Version of the Bible.

Scripture quotations marked "RSV" are from the Revised Standard Version of the Bible, copyright © 1946, 1952, and 1971 by the National Council of the Churches of Christ in the United States of America. Used by permission. All rights reserved.

Scripture quotations marked "NIV" are from the Holy Bible, New International Version®, NIV®, copyright © 1973, 1978, 1984, and 2011 by Biblica, Inc.™ Used by permission of Zondervan. All rights reserved worldwide.

Scripture quotations marked "NKJV" are from taken the New King James Version®. Copyright © 1982 by Thomas Nelson. Used by permission. All rights reserved.

Scripture quotations marked "NRSV" are from the New Revised Standard Bible, copyright © 1989 by the National Council of the Churches of Christ in the United States of America. Used by permission. All rights reserved.

Scripture quotations marked "ESV" are from the ESV® Bible (The Holy Bible, English Standard Version®), copyright © 2001 by Crossway, a publishing ministry of Good News Publishers. Used by permission. All rights reserved.

Because of the dynamic nature of the Internet, any web addresses or links contained in this book may have changed since publication and may no longer be valid.

Cover design by the author.
Stock imagery © Shutterstock.

The Nativity window on the cover was created by Franz Xaver Zettler (1841-1916) for The German Church (St. Gertrude's Church) in Stockholm, Sweden.

ISBN: 978-1-948773-06-5 (sc)

Library of Congress Control Number: 2018903096

To learn more about or purchase this or other works by Al Hill,
go to www.sommertonhouse.com,
or www.amazon.com/author/alhill.

Dedication

To my wife, Joanne,
who made the contents of this book possible;

first,
by challenging me
to begin writing out my sermons in full,

and then,
by allowing me to desert her every Saturday,
year after year,
as I secluded myself in the study to do so.

Contents

Dedication v
Preface ix

Sermons

The First Sunday in Advent
Chapter 1. **Understanding the Time** 5
Chapter 2. **Come Down, Lord!** 13
Chapter 3. **The Next Time He Comes…** 21
Chapter 4. **What Are You Waiting For?** 29
Chapter 5. **The Days Are Coming** 35

The Second Sunday in Advent
Chapter 6. **Here He Comes** 41
Chapter 7. **Patient Salvation** 47
Chapter 8. **And Along Come John** 53
Chapter 9. **God's Advance Man** 59

The Third Sunday in Advent
Chapter 10. **Is Jesus the One?** 67
Chapter 11. **Restore Our Fortunes** 73
Chapter 12. **God's Joy** 81
Chapter 13. **O Come, Let God Adore Us!** 89

The Fourth Sunday in Advent
Chapter 14. **The Christmas Problem** 95
Chapter 15. **Your Part in the Process** 103
Chapter 16. **Christmas Almost Didn't Happen** 109
Chapter 17. **The Lord is With You** 115
Chapter 18. **Impossible Child** 119
Chapter 19. **The One of Peace** 127
Chapter 20. **Magnify and Rejoice** 135

Christmas Eve
Chapter 21. **Where Are You Going for Christmas?** 145
Chapter 22. **The Christmas Story** 153
Chapter 23. **The Christmas Story (Abridged)** 159
Chapter 24. **The Time Came** 163
Chapter 25. **Come Closer** 169

Christmas Day
Chapter 26. **The Most Natural Thing in the World** 177
Chapter 27. **Born Today** 183
Chapter 28. **Unto Us a Son is Given** 189
Chapter 29. **In the Flesh** 195
Chapter 30. **God Like Us** 199

Sunday After Christmas
Chapter 31. **Born that Men No More May Die** 207
Chapter 32. **What Did You Get for Christmas?** 215
Chapter 33. **What's Got into That Boy?** 223
Chapter 34. **Looking for Jesus—Finding the Christ** 227

Epiphany
Chapter 35. **Going a Different Way** 239
Chapter 36. **Journey's End** 247

Indices
Sermon Titles in Alphabetical Order 254
Sermon Texts in Biblical Order 256
Sermon Texts in Lectionary Order 259
Additional Scriptures Referenced 262

Preface

This is a book of sermons.
Yes, another one.
And why?

Because, though "Christmas Comes but Once a Year," it does come—every year. And every year, amid the hubbub of the holiday season, those who have the privilege and responsibility to preach the story of the Coming of Christ must find ways to present the good but familiar news with the power and wonder and depth it deserves to people whose response will determine how they will live their lives—and where they will spend eternity.

This collection of sermons is offered, first of all, as a collaborative Christmas gift to other preachers, both military and civilian, who are preparing messages for their people in the very busy weeks between Thanksgiving and New Year's. Perhaps what I have written will suggest some new perspective or enhance an old one. Perhaps I can save you some time if, like me, you find preparing sermons a painfully slow process.

For everybody else, some sermon in the collection may provide a new appreciation of the age-old events we rehearse and celebrate at the end (or beginning, ecclesiastically) of each year. There may be something in these pages that will make your personal experience of these events—and of the Christ Who came—and still comes—at Christmas, more meaningful.

The sermons in this collection were all written to be heard by people—rather than to be read by them. This is the reason for some oddities in syntax and punctuation, which my very conscientious editor could not convince me to amend.[1] The sermons were preached over a period of 15 years in two Navy chapels and two civilian churches, all of which were interdenominational in makeup. Some references to people and current events will "date" some sermons. In defense, I point out that even Luke set his story in its historical context. Sermons are intended to speak eternal truth to people in the ever evaporating present. And it occurred to me that if I attempted to alter the sermons to bring details "up-to-date," it would not be long before my "modernizations" would themselves be "out-of-date."

Some of the sermons here were related to others preached before and after them in a particular year, as will be apparent when you read them. The published order of the sermons in this book has made the original connections between sermons less obvious because the collection has been arbitrarily re-arranged (as a favor to other preachers) according to the relationship of texts to the Revised Common Lectionary, first in terms of the week or day in Advent or Christmastide they appear, and then according to the annual "Cycles"—A, B and C. (The basic Gospel texts for Christmas Eve and Christmas Day—Luke 2 and John 1—are the same for all three years.)

---

[1] I know that the current convention is *not* to capitalize "divine pronouns," but I have chosen to reject this convention in my sermons, though I honor it when reproducing the various copyrighted versions of the texts upon which the sermons were based. In addition, you will find some unusually long and convoluted sentences. I preached them that way, and have left them as I preached them (mostly). The benefit of having the written text before you is that even though you cannot hear the inflection in my voice, you can reread a sentence if you didn't understand it the first time. And yes, there are "em-dashes" everywhere. Sometimes, a comma is just not enough to suggest the speech pattern employed—and the nuance of meaning intended. Well, you get the point.

All of the sermons are intended to be closely controlled by the scripture upon which they're based. I try to focus on what the biblical text actually says and what those words may be reasonably understood to mean or suggest. You will decide for yourself whether a sermon has been faithful to that intent.

Over the years—and in different congregations—different versions of the Bible were used "in the pews." That criteria determined the text of a particular sermon, which is important because the specific wording of each translation colored what was said in a sermon preached in that place. For that reason, I have gone to the trouble to indicate the version of the text used in each sermon and encourage you to consult it. Unfortunately, the 1984 edition of the New International Version is no longer available for publication, and so sermons based originally on that edition of the Bible are noted under the titles, while what is actually printed in the book before the sermon is the text of the English Standard Version. When scriptures other than the text have been quoted—or biblical events alluded to—in the body of a sermon, references (that were not a part of the oral presentation, of course) have been provided without concern for version.

Most of the sermons are "full length" efforts. A few, which were preached in liturgical communion services, are shorter homilies. "The Christmas Story," for instance, was preached first as a sermon and later edited and preached to a different congregation as one of these briefer homilies.

The last two sermons are based on Matthew 2:1-12, the story of the Magi, a text that properly belongs, according to the Lectionary, to Epiphany. But because the Wise Men and their guiding star are such a central part of the popular "composition" of Christmas, I have included these sermons in this Advent/Christmas collection. Two sermons are drawn from the lone childhood episode of Jesus, which, though not actually a "Christmas story," does appear on the Sunday after Christmas in the Lectionary.

As you read through the sermons, you may notice concepts and perspectives recurring, sometimes as the major emphasis, at other times, as minor, supportive themes. This should be expected of a single, limited mind, even if the Holy Spirit is to some degree advising and supervising the process of preparation. However, each year as Advent approached, I tried to take a fresh look at the familiar story and find some new way to enter into it. The Bible in general—and the Christmas Story in particular—contain countless treasures of divine revelation whose full extent and value can never be fully mined or measured.

If you are reading this book, then you and I likely have something very significant in common. We are "Christmas people." We are like the shepherds who heard the angels and beheld this gracious, glorious Gift of God. We were told what God was doing, and we came to the place where Jesus was, and found that what we had been told—that He was our Savior—was true. And from that time on, we have experienced life differently.

But even more than the shepherds, we are like Mary and Joseph, who made Jesus their own when they really didn't know what that meant—and lived with Him and loved Him and experienced His love for them every day. Every day, we are the family of Jesus. Every day, we live our lives with Him, remembering, amid whatever is happening, what happened when He came into our lives that first special day.

We are Christmas people. Wherever we are, we will go in our spirits this and every Christmas season to Bethlehem, to await and worship the Holy Child. And we will not leave Christmas without Him, because He has been born to us. For you and me and all Christmas people, the reality and spirit of Christmas endures.

And I hope that, in some small way, my witness to the wonder of Christmas in these pages will make your Christmas more wonderful, too.

Sermons

The First Sunday in Advent

1.

Understanding the Time

Romans 13:11-14 ESV

¹¹...you know the time, that the hour has come for you to wake from sleep. For salvation is nearer to us now than when we first believed. ¹² The night is far gone; the day is at hand. So then let us cast off the works of darkness and put on the armor of light. ¹³ Let us walk properly as in the daytime, not in orgies and drunkenness, not in sexual immorality and sensuality, not in quarreling and jealousy. ¹⁴ But put on the Lord Jesus Christ, and make no provision for the flesh, to gratify its desires.

※

I would like to begin the sermon with a little experiment today. Would you help me? Those of you listening on the radio are welcome to participate at home. If you're listening in the car, just drive; this could get complicated.

First of all, will those of you who are left-handed, please raise your right hand? It's all right; you're not voting for anything or enlisting in the service. Leave your hands up for a moment. Now, will the right-handers please raise your left hand? Good. Now, notice how many of these uplifted arms have wristwatches attached to them.

Understanding the Time

We are a people determined to know what time it is, at any second, down to the second. We wear these watches so we can check the time, anytime. If you take a quick look, you will all know the time, right now. Thank you, you can put your hands—and your watches—down.

I know it's probably not wise for a preacher to call your attention to the time at the beginning of a sermon. I hope you won't feel the need to look at your watches again—at least until I'm finished. If you do, I'll have nobody to blame but myself, I guess.

※

What was the purpose of this little exercise? The purpose was to make a point—and a distinction. The point is that we are a group of Christians who know the time—with pinpoint accuracy. And the distinction? That the kind of time we've been talking about is not the kind of time Paul is talking about in the passage you heard earlier.

Paul wrote to the Christians in Rome almost two thousand years ago. They had no Rolexes or Timexes or Seikos. With their sundials and hourglasses, they were lucky if they could tell the difference between "quarter after" and "ten till."

Furthermore, there were no time zones—no Daylight-Saving Time—no standardization of time measurement from one country to the next—or even one village to the next. Paul's letter to the Roman Christians would have taken weeks—perhaps months—to get from him to them. He would have no way of knowing what time it would be when they received it or read it out to the group.

But Paul assumed they knew the time. He didn't know them; he'd never been to Rome. But they were Christians and so he could write to them with confidence that they knew the time. Paul assumed that to be a Christian means you know something about time that those who have not believed in Jesus don't know.

So, do you know the time? Do you? Or are you finding yourself a little hazy on the subject just now?

I mentioned a moment ago a distinction: Paul is talking about time, but it is a different kind of time. He is even using a different word. The word for "tick-tick-tick" time—the time on your watch (don't look, just trust me on this), that word is *"chronos."* That's why Navy clocks are called "chronometers" and a listing of things in the time sequence they happened is called a "chronology."

But there is another kind of time—a special, "not-like-time" time—a time when time stands still or has nothing to do with the passage of that *chronos* time. We sense it when babies are born or wedding vows are spoken. There's a sense of it in the worst moments of war and the holiest moments of worship. There is another time—sometimes intersecting the mundane, everyday *chronos* time—sometimes arching far above and beyond it. It is God's time.

Paul calls it *"kairos."* And it is everything that *chronos* is not. *Chronos* time moves with the certainty of the tides and waits for no man. *Kairos* time, on the other hand, has the patience of God and is so tied to eternity that God has all the time—not merely "in the world"—but in all the worlds in all Creation, and in the infinity of space between and around and beyond all those worlds.

Chronos time is the time it takes for animal, vegetable or mineral to get from Point A to Point B. *Chronos* time is measurable; *kairos* time is not—it's miraculous. *Kairos* time is the time it takes for God to restore His fallen Creation and to draw your sinful heart to Him. *Kairos* is the time it takes for a Messiah to be born in a manger and to die on a Cross and to rise from the dead. It's a different kind of time: it's God's time.

Of course, *kairos* time is so different from *chronos* time that a lot of people don't realize that such a thing exists. You can tell them there's a time unlike our time and, a lot of times, they just won't believe it. They don't know the time—the *kairos* time.

But you do—if you're a Christian. The time you became a Christian was *kairos* time. You may remember the hour and day, the place and the circumstances, the *chronos* details. But the moment when you meet Jesus is a *kairos* moment—always. It only happens in God's time.

The time you spend with Jesus is *kairos* time, even if you measure it off in the minutes and hours of *chronos*. God's time and our time intersect, but they are never the same.

They are so different, in fact, that it's like the difference between being awake and being asleep. You can cruise through your life on autopilot, oblivious to some or all of what's going on around you or within you. You can devote your life to a detailed schedule or leave it to fate to fill in the hours of your day. But if you're not paying attention to that other kind of time—that *kairos* time—you're not really cruizin'; you're snoozin'.

That's why Paul says, *"You know the time."* You've met Jesus. You've experienced the Holy Spirit coming into you. You've stepped into *kairos* time for a moment. Don't forget it—or ignore it—or let it pass you by. You know there is a *kairos* time—God's time. Don't get distracted by *chronos* time and everything that happens there. *Chronos* is just our way of going from Point A to B to C. Wake up to what God is doing in His special, eternal time.

Once you have met Jesus, you can live in both times, not just one. But to do this, to spend *kairos* time with Jesus, not just *chronos* time studying or thinking about Him—going through the motions—you must go beyond *knowing* the time to *understanding* the time—understanding that there is a reality where you spend your life in the presence of God and in loving relationship with Him. To live your life with the holy One Who has given you life, you have to wake up from your *chronos* life to the *kairos* life.

༄༅

Sometimes, when I'm all warm and comfortable and not really paying attention to things, I've been known to nod off. One minute I'm awake and the next I'm asleep and I don't even realize it until I start to slip and I startle myself back to consciousness. Some of you may be having that same experience right now.

Paul says, "Wake up! You know about *kairos* time. You understand what it is. You've been there with Jesus. It's not just something that happened 'way back when,' one day in *chronos* time."

It's God time all the time: when God saved you, and every time God speaks to you and blesses you and reaches out to touch your life. It's your special time with God now. And God wants it to be all the time, and it can be, if you don't slip back into the other time where nobody thinks about God's time or even knows it exists.

Chronos and *kairos* are as different as night and day. But Paul says the night is just about over; the day is about to dawn.

So, get up, you spiritual sleepy head! Rise and shine and give God the glory! Throw off the dark deeds of your *chronos* time like a blanket that's in the way and jump into God's *kairos* reality like a new set of clothes.

If you get focused on this world—this time—all you'll do is *chronos* stuff. Punch the clock. Do your job. Get ahead if you can. Have a little fun. Hang on till you die.

But if you understand the *kairos*—the reality of God's time and its fullness revealed in Jesus Christ—you can put on, not just the armor of light God has given you for this time, but the very essence of the Lord Himself. *Kairos* and *chronos* are worlds apart—as far apart as this world is from the next.

Or at least you would think they were, if you didn't know and understand about *kairos* time. If you know anything about *kairos*—understand anything about this miraculous time when the reality of God and His eternity entangles itself in love and grace with the plodding predictability of our time—you know that it's so close *all* the time that you can reach out and touch it—or rather that God can (and does) reach out of it and touch you and take your hand

and lead you into His sacred and supernatural time, if you will let Him.

❧

How do you tell people about *kairos* when they only know *chronos*—only understand *chronos*—only believe *chronos*?

You tell them about things that happened when God placed a *kairos* moment alongside a *chronos* one. Three of our members did that on Wednesday night when they testified to God's generosity in their lives—and the gratitude they were able to reach across time and give Him. The Anderson family added a *kairos* moment to our *chronos* time this morning as they lit a Candle of Hope in our seemingly hopeless world.

And we will all point to the *kairos* time of God over the next few weeks when we repeat the story we have settled securely into our chronological calendars: the story of a *kairos* moment when a virgin gave birth to a Baby and angels sang and shepherds wondered and wise men came and worshipped. Old story—new truth. On a day like any other and like no other, two times came together—*chronos* and *kairos*—and the heaven of God touched the world of mankind.

Tell them that, if they do not understand the time. Tell them God's salvation is even closer to us—now—than when we first believed. And it can be just as close to them.

Well, time's up—for the sermon, I mean. It has a chronological limit. But the *message* of this sermon is a part of God's *kairos* time. The message will keep on going—in the timeless time of God—if you tell it.

The First Sunday in Advent

Isaiah (63:15-19, Optional Additional Text); 64:1-9 NRSV

*(**63**^{15} Look down from heaven and see,*
 from your holy and glorious habitation.
Where are your zeal and your might?
 The yearning of your heart and your compassion?
 They are withheld from me.
^{16} For you are our father,
 though Abraham does not know us
 and Israel does not acknowledge us;
you, O LORD, *are our father;*
 our Redeemer from of old is your name.
^{17} Why, O LORD, *do you make us stray from your ways*
 and harden our heart, so that we do not fear you?
Turn back for the sake of your servants,
 for the sake of the tribes that are your heritage.
^{18} Your holy people took possession for a little while;
 but now our adversaries have trampled down your sanctuary.
^{19} We have long been like those whom you do not rule,
 like those not called by your name.)

64^{1} *O that you would tear open the heavens and come down,*
 so that the mountains would quake at your presence—
^{2} as when fire kindles brushwood
 and the fire causes water to boil—
to make your name known to your adversaries,
 so that the nations might tremble at your presence!
^{3} When you did awesome deeds that we did not expect,
 you came down, the mountains quaked at your presence.
^{4} From ages past no one has heard,
 no ear has perceived,
no eye has seen any God besides you,
 who works for those who wait for him.

⁵ You meet those who gladly do right,
   those who remember you in your ways.
But you were angry, and we sinned;
   because you hid yourself we transgressed.
⁶ We have all become like one who is unclean,
   and all our righteous deeds are like a filthy cloth.
We all fade like a leaf,
   and our iniquities, like the wind, take us away.
⁷ There is no one who calls on your name,
   or attempts to take hold of you;
for you have hidden your face from us,
   and have delivered us into the hand of our iniquity.
⁸ Yet, O LORD, you are our Father;
   we are the clay, and you are our potter;
   we are all the work of your hand.
⁹ Do not be exceedingly angry, O LORD,
   and do not remember iniquity forever.
   Now consider, we are all your people.

2.

Come Down, Lord!

Isaiah (63:15-19 and) 64:1-9, NRSV

I wonder what God has planned for Christmas this year. We all have plans for Christmas. We all have things we intend to do. I wonder what God has in mind.

While we're putting up our decorations and attending our parties—while we're going to see family or waiting for them to come here, what will God be doing, up there in heaven?

Have you given it any thought—what God will be doing? Do you care what God will be doing, up there in heaven? Not that we would ignore God—not at Christmastime. We'll sing His praises and tell the story of His Nativity. But that's all about what He *did*. What do you think He's going to do *now*?

Or more to the point, what do you want Him to do now? We all want things for Christmas. We're making lists and checking them twice. Oh wait, that's Santa Claus. But we do the same thing. We let our wants run rampant and try to satisfy the wants of others—those we love, and even some we don't love, but simply want to impress or butter up. Our whole economy is based on generating and satisfying want.

Is there anything you want from God—right now? What do you want God to do?

The prophet Isaiah had something he wanted God to do.

"Oh that you would tear open the heavens and come down!" he said. "Oh, that You would come down here and knock down some mountains and set some things on fire! Oh, that You would get right in the face of Your enemies and scare the 'bejebees' out of them."

Now I don't know exactly what "bejebees" are, but I get the sense that if they are scared out of you, you have been significantly scared.

"Oh, that You would come down," says Isaiah, "and do the kind of awesome and terrifying things that You used to do."

That's what Isaiah wanted God to do for Christmas, five hundred years and more before the first Christmas. "Come down out of heaven and do something big, awesome, earth shaking, nation shaking, people shaking. Come do something like You did before. Come down, Lord, and change the world—'cause we can't stand it the way it is."

Isaiah knows his history. You see, God has a track record. He comes down—out of heaven. And when He does, He lights a fire somewhere.

God came down at the very beginning and tore open the primal chaos and created everything—land and light and us.[2] He came down again and tore open the Red Sea to bring His chosen people out of bondage,[3] and burned a path for them with a fiery pillar[4] through the desert to Mount Sinai where He carved out commandments[5] and a destiny for them as His children.[6]

God came down and knocked down the walls of Jericho so they could take the land He promised them.[7] He came down and knocked down a giant named Goliath so that a shepherd boy

---

[2] Genesis 1.
[3] Exodus 14.
[4] Exodus 13:17-22.
[5] Exodus 20:1-17.
[6] Exodus 19:1-6.
[7] Joshua 6.

named David could become a king.[8] God came down with a fire that burned wood and sacrifice and the water Elijah had poured over them at Mount Carmel to prove there was no god like this God.[9] This is a God Who comes down in power and changes the world.

This is a God that Isaiah calls out to, in the face of death and destruction and despair. There is no help, no hope, no possibility of salvation from the disasters of his day—except that this God come down out of heaven.

That is what Isaiah wants from God because that is what Isaiah—and the desperate and defeated people of God—need from God.

They want what they must have. And so they pray—Isaiah's words—their deepest desire: "Come down, Lord. Shake your world and show Your enemies (and our tormentors) what Your power is really like."

We tend to say, "Okay, Lord, thanks for the salvation and all, but we can handle it from here." And all the while, the enemies of God are on the march. Our sinful self-reliance is killing us. Read your papers. Watch the news. Look around.

I'm not here to preach the headlines, but they certainly demonstrate that the world is turning away from God. People have become content with a comfortable and undemanding materialism—or obsessed with visions or creeds that compel them to impose some system of behavior on everyone, by deception, coercion or violence, if necessary.

"Come down, Lord, and turn things around. Come down and make this world different."

"Make us different."

Isaiah understood the problem. His plea for God's power and presence is accompanied by confession. What the world (and God's people) need most from God they deserve not at all. And

---

[8] 1 Samuel 17.
[9] 1 Kings 18:20-40.

many in the world want God's intervention not at all. If God does not come down and defeat His enemies and protect His people—if He does not pour out His power on those who are His children—what are His children to do?

God coming down from heaven is an awesome, terrifying thing. But His *not* coming down is far worse. The only thing more terrifying than the presence of God is the absence of God. For God to hide Himself is like the sun going dark and the moon not shining—like the stars falling out of the sky. For those who know God, life without Him is unbearable.

Paul tells the Romans that God's ultimate punishment is to give sinful men up to their own perverse and wicked will.[10] Because they choose to live in the shadows, God will give them that and more: darkness—the absence of light.

They may not notice the light going out at first—they have done so much to avoid it. They do not call on God's Name (except as profanity). They do not attempt to take hold of God (except to hold Him up to ridicule and derision) and so, finally, they discover they have been delivered by their deeds and attitudes into the hand of their own iniquity.

But we acclimate ourselves. We adjust. Today, despite our scientific splendors and our technical marvels, we live in a moral and spiritual twilight we could not have imagined possible—let alone acceptable—a generation ago. The Light fades when the world rejects It and all the world is cast into darkness. God hides His face and we are lost in the very world He has given us.

And one day, when you've had enough, you cry out. When you cannot stand the darkness any longer and have no power in yourself to overcome it, you pray to the God Who can tear the heavens open and come down—come down and light up the world. It's all you can do.

---

[10] Romans 1:18-32.

The First Sunday in Advent

Sometime in the month ahead, you'll probably hear a cheery little song singing:

> "We need a little Christmas—
> right this very minute…"[11]

Don't be fooled. It's not true. We don't need a *little* Christmas—a few weeks of peace and good will while the presents are purchased, wrapped, opened and forgotten.

We need a heaven-full of Christmas—all there is—and we need it not just now—for a fleeting moment in time—but for all eternity. Oh, that God would rip heaven wide open and come down—and bring earthquake and fire so that people would experience His presence and power in a way that would drive them all to their knees—friend and foe alike.

You see, not all who are turning away from God are outside the Church. Not all who reject God's claim upon them renounce the Name He has given to them. And so we pray for God's appearance (if we do) as a people divided—a Church that is sinful: spiritually weak and morally unclean.

Two thousand years after the ultimate answer to Isaiah's prayer, we still pray it, and all the more for being divided, weak, and sinful. We pray for God's return from heaven, because we have seen the power of His leaving heaven to confront His enemies face to face with a face—a human face—like theirs. We have felt the fire He kindles in the hearts of those who will let Him melt the mountain of opposition within their hearts.

And we know that God is not done coming down with power to save His children, and defeat His enemies, and demonstrate to all that He remains the incomparable God.

What do you think God will do this Christmas? What do you want Him to do? You know what He's done in the past. You know what the world is like.

---

[11] From "We Need a Little Christmas," Jerry Herman, composer (for the Broadway musical, *Mame*), 1966.

Come Down, Lord

Christmas can be very pleasant this year. We can make it so. But for Christmas to be powerful—for it to be life-changing and world-changing—God's going to have to take over the process—again—and come down. He's done it before. He can do it again.

You can "deck the halls with boughs of holly"[12]—or you can pray that "the power of the Lord comes down."[13] Seeing a few mountains—or a few nations—tremble before our God—seeing a few rebellious children call on His name and reach out to lay hold of Him—that would make it a Christmas to remember.

Come down, Lord.

---

[12] From "Deck the Halls," English lyrics by Thomas Oliphant, 1862.
[13] From "Now Let Us Sing," a traditional spiritual.

Mark 13:24-37 ESV

[Jesus said:]
   ^{24} "But in those days, after that tribulation, the sun will be darkened, and the moon will not give its light, ^{25} and the stars will be falling from heaven, and the powers in the heavens will be shaken. ^{26} And then they will see the Son of Man coming in clouds with great power and glory. ^{27} And then he will send out the angels and gather his elect from the four winds, from the ends of the earth to the ends of heaven.
   ^{28} "From the fig tree learn its lesson: as soon as its branch becomes tender and puts out its leaves, you know that summer is near. ^{29} So also, when you see these things taking place, you know that he is near, at the very gates. ^{30} Truly, I say to you, this generation will not pass away until all these things take place. ^{31} Heaven and earth will pass away, but my words will not pass away.
   ^{32} "But concerning that day or that hour, no one knows, not even the angels in heaven, nor the Son, but only the Father. ^{33} Be on guard, keep awake. For you do not know when the time will come. ^{34} It is like a man going on a journey, when he leaves home and puts his servants in charge, each with his work, and commands the doorkeeper to stay awake. ^{35} Therefore stay awake—for you do not know when the master of the house will come, in the evening, or at midnight, or when the rooster crows, or in the morning— ^{36} lest he come suddenly and find you asleep. ^{37} And what I say to you I say to all: Stay awake."

3.

The Next Time He Comes

Mark 13:24-37 ESV

Each year about this time, we Christians turn our attention to the coming of our Lord. We celebrate the birth of Jesus Christ at the end of each year and, if we are lucky—or extremely disciplined—we can separate our spiritual, devotional efforts, to some degree, from the increasingly crass and commercial activities whirling around us as our modern, secular world fiercely pursues its uninformed idea of Christmas.

Yes, we buy gifts, too, and give them. We decorate our houses and hang stockings on our hearths. We get together with loved ones, if we can, and we look forward, as much as anyone, to the raptured look on little faces when they wake up on Christmas morn.

But having offered our thanksgiving to God for His bounty and the blessings of the year, we Christians remain painfully aware that, even with all God's grace poured out upon us, we are still living out our lives in a terribly broken world. Though we have been redeemed by the Blood of the Lamb, we ourselves have not yet been released from the lure of temptation and our capacity for sin. We long for the fulfillment of the miracle of our salvation. The foretaste of glory we have been granted leaves us yearning for the divine feast that is to come—that awaits us in heaven as we await—here on earth—our Risen Lord's return.

We await our Lord's Second Coming because we have experienced the power and glory made possible in our lives by His First Coming. And each year, we remember the promise of His return and turn our attention, not to presents and parties, but to things like hope and peace and joy and divine love, holy gifts that are part of the sacred covenant we have entered into with God through His Son.

We live between the First Coming and the Second Coming. The First has made the Second possible. The Second will complete the First. They are both essential parts of God's plan of salvation.

Throughout this Advent season, we will rehearse and reflect upon the familiar figures and scenes of that first Christmas: Mary and Joseph, angels and shepherds, the stable and the star, and the birth of God's Messiah in a borrowed manger. Humble and heartwarming, the story of His coming inspires and encourages us, year after year as we live in faith and wait—for the next time He comes.

But today, the Bible bids us focus on that "next time." The followers of Jesus asked Him about that next time, and this is what He said, *"...they will see the Son of Man coming in clouds with great power and glory. And then he will send the angels and they will assemble his chosen out of the four winds, from the farthest end of earth to the farthest end of heaven."*

There won't be many churches incorporating *this* scene into their Christmas pageants this year, I suspect. But we might do well to break it down a little bit and reflect on what, for us, may be the *less* familiar figures and scenes of the Second Advent of our Lord.

According to Jesus, the next time He comes, *"they will see [him] coming—in clouds—with great power—and glory."*

Who are "they?" Who, exactly, (does He say) will see Him?

The original wording is not as precise as the translation we read implies. If you read all of Mark 13 carefully, it appears Jesus means the Chosen—the believers He is coming to claim. And that much is certainly to be expected, for John writes in his first epistle, *"...we know that when he appears, we shall be like him, for we shall see him as he is."*[14]

On the other hand, it may very well be that Jesus is referring to everybody, those who believed in Him and those who did not, for Paul says that *every* knee will bow to Jesus and *every* tongue will confess that He is Lord.[15] They have not done so yet, but they will. And what is more likely to evoke that submissive response than seeing Jesus as He describes, *"coming in clouds"*—the next time He comes?

Of course, to be precise, Jesus says, *"they will see the Son of Man coming in clouds."* But don't let the title confuse you. "The Son of Man" is how Jesus refers to Himself in the New Testament. He probably borrowed the title from the Old Testament prophet Ezekiel, who used it frequently during a ministry that brought nothing but ridicule and rejection for preaching God's word. It would have made sense that Jesus, Whose words were received like Ezekiel's had been centuries before, would describe Himself in the same way.

But more than that, Jesus also had the vision of Daniel to draw on to describe His Second Coming. *"...I looked,"* wrote Daniel, *"and there before me was one like a son of man, coming with the clouds of heaven."*[16] It will be just like Daniel says, Jesus told them, the next time I come.

And how different from the first time! The first time, Jesus came in a cow stall.[17] The next time He comes, He will come in great power and glory. The first time He came, He did not have the power even to raise His own head off His mother's chest or

---

[14] 1 John 3:2, RSV.
[15] Philippians 2:10-11.
[16] Daniel 7:13.
[17] See the second stanza of the hymn, "I Wonder as I Wander," John Jacob Niles, 1933.

roll Himself over in the manger. The first time He came, Jesus had all the apparent glory of a soiled diaper or a newborn's single-minded focus on His first meal.

If the angels had not sung His glory to the shepherds, and the shepherds had not gossiped it to whoever they ran into after leaving the stable, Mary and Joseph would have been the only people in the world with even a clue.

But the next time He comes, Jesus will come with great power—enough power to raise all the dead who ever lived. He will come with enough power to reconstitute every body that ever drew breath—plus all those that should have, but never got the chance. He will come with enough power to transform the body of every believer from its perishable, mortal, physical nature to a body that is imperishable, immortal and spiritual. Jesus will come with enough power to do this for all our bodies—instantly, simultaneously, permanently and perfectly.[18] He will come with great power, the next time He comes.

The first time He came, Jesus emptied Himself of every bit of glory that was His by divine right. He came to be *"despised and rejected...a man of sorrows, acquainted with grief."*[19] The next time He comes, He will come in all His Father's glory.

That kind of glory is hard to imagine, but there are those who have tried. Long before Julia Ward Howe wrote the first line of *The Battle Hymn of the Republic*,[20] the John of the Revelation showed that *his* eyes had seen the glory of the coming of the Lord. He wrote,

"I saw heaven standing open and there before me was a white horse, whose rider is called Faithful and True. With justice he judges and makes war. His eyes are like blazing fire, and on his head are many crowns. He has a name written on him that no one knows but he himself. He is dressed in a robe dipped in blood, and his name is the Word of God. The armies of heaven were following him, riding on white horses and dressed in fine linen, white and clean.

---

[18] 1 Corinthians 15:35-53.
[19] Isaiah 53:3, RSV.
[20] "The Battle Hymn of the Republic," Julia Ward Howe, November 1861.

The First Sunday in Advent

Out of his mouth comes a sharp sword with which to strike down the nations. He will rule them with an iron scepter. He treads the winepress of the fury of the wrath of God Almighty. On his robe and on his thigh he has this name written: 'KING OF KINGS AND LORD OF LORDS.'"[21]

The next time He comes, it will be with great power and glory.

❧❦

And then He will send the angels.

The first time Jesus came, God sent angels to announce His birth to the shepherding night shift and to start the still ongoing celebration of His humble Incarnation. Later, God sent angels to minister to Jesus after He withstood the devil's temptations in the desert.

The next time He comes, Jesus will command the angels Himself. He will send the angels in all the directions of the compass, like mighty winds over every inch of earth. He will send angels to the farthest corners of heaven.

They will go, not to sing His praises, or even to serve His needs, but to summon every believer to Him. His angels will bring every dead believer's body from the farthest reaches of land and sea, no matter where it ended up. His angels will bring every believer's soul from wherever in heaven it has been resting in peace and waiting to be reunited with its body in the resurrection. And then the angels will bring every believer still alive. And all together, we will come to Him. The angels will go forth and bring every one of His Chosen—every Christian—to the all-glorious and all-powerful Christ.

But the angels will not merely "bring" us. They will "assemble" us, according to the original wording. The angels will organize every one of us so that we are exactly *where* we are supposed to be and exactly *what* we are supposed to be. Jesus told His disciples He was going to prepare a place for us so that where He is, there we

---
[21] Revelation 19:11-16.

The Next Time He Comes

may be also.[22] And the next time He comes, He will send the angels to ensure that every one of us is in our proper place, the place Jesus prepared, lovingly, for us.

Today, we light the Candle of Hope and remember the first time Jesus came to earth. To take a line from our communion liturgy: "It is meet and right so to do."[23] It is right for us to tell the story of the birth of Jesus, to sing the familiar carols and put on that warm Christmas spirit like a comfortable old sweater. It is right to do, because His coming that first Christmas brought with Him our redemption, our salvation, our hope. The First Coming of Jesus provides the hope for His Second Coming. All the wonders of that Christmas are spiritual gifts to sustain us as we await His Return.

Because of His Coming, His "is the kingdom and the power and the glory forever and ever." And ours is the knowledge that, the next time He comes, *we* will be the beloved children who awake on that glorious morning with the wide-eyed look of amazement and joy.

---

[22] John 14:1-3.
[23] From *The Episcopal Book of Common Prayer*, 1928.

Jeremiah 33:14-16 NRSV

^{14} The days are surely coming, says the LORD, when I will fulfill the promise I made to the house of Israel and the house of Judah. ^{15} In those days and at that time I will cause a righteous Branch to spring up for David; and he shall execute justice and righteousness in the land. ^{16} In those days Judah will be saved and Jerusalem will live in safety. And this is the name by which it will be called: "The LORD is our righteousness."

What Are You Waiting For?

Luke 21:25-36 ESV

[Jesus said:]

[25] "And there will be signs in sun and moon and stars, and on the earth distress of nations in perplexity because of the roaring of the sea and the waves, [26] people fainting with fear and with foreboding of what is coming on the world. For the powers of the heavens will be shaken. [27] And then they will see the Son of Man coming in a cloud with power and great glory. [28] Now when these things begin to take place, straighten up and raise your heads, because your redemption is drawing near."

[29] And he told them a parable: "Look at the fig tree, and all the trees. [30] As soon as they come out in leaf, you see for yourselves and know that the summer is already near. [31] So also, when you see these things taking place, you know that the kingdom of God is near. [32] Truly, I say to you, this generation will not pass away until all has taken place. [33] Heaven and earth will pass away, but my words will not pass away.

[34] "But watch yourselves lest your hearts be weighed down with dissipation and drunkenness and cares of this life, and that day come upon you suddenly like a trap. [35] For it will come upon all who dwell on the face of the whole earth. [36] But stay awake at all times, praying that you may have strength to escape all these things that are going to take place, and to stand before the Son of Man."

[37] And every day he was teaching in the temple, but at night he went out and lodged on the mount called Olivet. [38] And early in the morning all the people came to him in the temple to hear him.

4.

What Are You Waiting For?

Jeremiah 33:14-16; Luke 21:25-36 ESV

Late on Thanksgiving Day, after all the eating was done—or, at least, most of it—many people left the comfort of their recliners to stand resolutely in the ranks of strangers, braving the cold and darkness, waiting—often for hours—for something (they believed) would make their wait worthwhile.

I know this to be true. I watched it myself on TV—from the comfort of my recliner.

Other people—fueled by a similar form of fanaticism, did not go out before going to bed, but, instead, rose from their slumber deep in the night to fulfill dreams that had come to them while fully awake. They formed the second wave of "waiters," lined up and poised to charge toward their targets, even before the dawn of day, at the moment they saw the signal to advance.

I know this to be true. It was recorded and replayed for me to watch when I got up—leisurely and later than usual—on Friday morning.

What were all these people waiting for?

The opportunity to enter a place where what they wanted could be had for far less than it was worth. They were waiting for sales—*bargains*—STEALS—*THE DEAL OF A LIFETIME!* And this was the day—the one fleeting chance—to make these particular dreams come true.

In some locations, the doors opened at midnight, and so folks went out when they would normally have gone to bed. Other places opened at first light—or before—and so seemingly normal human beings became nocturnal animals.

What happened when the doors were opened and the waiting was over?

The ABCs of Black Friday: Anarchy—Bedlam—Chaos. Ordinarily civilized people—or nearly so—showed their savage side as they raced and wrestled for what many wanted and few could have.

For many of these people, the wait will not have been worth it. This will be true even for some of those who were actually able to get one of whatever they were waiting for. In this world, "things" often disappoint. They break or wear out in time. They may be stolen. Sometimes, they simply don't live up to their build-up from the beginning. Many things in this world aren't worth the wait.

And yet, we're all waiting. We all live our lives waiting for something, whether we realize it or not. We wait for "what's next," if nothing else—for the future—something we may be able to anticipate, to a degree, but which we can never predict with any degree of accuracy.

If you grow impatient with the process and say, like a little child awaiting a birthday or Christmas or the last day of school, "I can't wait!" life will answer you as your parent probably did, "Well, you'll just have to." Every day of our lives, we're waiting.

And what are we waiting for?

Oh, the usual things: we're waiting to grow up—to go to school and then to get done with it. We're waiting to meet the right person and land the right job. We're waiting for "things to work out" and success to come our way. In time, we're waiting to retire so we can finally do the things we want to do, and then, when we can't do much of anything anymore, we're waiting to die.

And along the way, we're waiting for countless little things that seem unbearably important for a while—until we get them—or realize we never will. And then we wonder why we thought they were ever worth waiting for in the first place.

But all the while that we are waiting for all that other stuff, we are really waiting for something far greater—something so great, most people cannot see it at all. We are waiting for the coming of Christ.

Every person born into this world lives whatever time he or she has, under whatever circumstances, with whatever results (from a worldly perspective), and along the way, and at the end, there is always something lacking in the ledger—thanks to sin. Our lives never become fully what they should have been—what we sense or suspect they could have been if the world had been a different place, and we—all of us—had been different people.

But the world is what it is—and we are who we are—and if that is not to be the last word on the subject—Someone else must come and write a different one for us. Christ must come and write of our lives: "Finally—and forever—made right." And whether you know it or not, that's what all of us are waiting for.

And we've been waiting a long, long time. Centuries before the birth of Jesus, prophets like Jeremiah looked through the eyes of God at their messed-up world and saw a Messiah making His way to earth. "One day—" they said—God said—"One day, this disappointing dynasty of David's will produce a king who can get the job done—who can do what God—and we—want done, in terms of justice and righteousness. That's a promise! One day I will send One Who will save you from yourself and your world and make you safe, not just for now—or the rest of your life on earth—but for all eternity."

And so, they waited—those who heard this word from God and believed it. They waited throughout their lives—till the day they died—as did generations who came after them. The faithful were waiting in pastures for the promised Messiah when He was born in a Bethlehem stable nearby,[24] and they were waiting in the Temple precincts in Jerusalem when that newborn Baby's parents brought Him there to dedicate Him to the work of making all the world's waiting worthwhile.[25]

And this Baby—God incarnate—also waited—until He grew into manhood[26]—until He heard the divine calling to begin His life's work[27]—until His enemies came in the night and took Him to be nailed the next day to a cross[28]—until life left His battered human Body[29]—until God the Father came on the third day to raise God the Son from death to life eternal[30] and prove that His sacred promise would be kept—and that all the waiting was worthwhile.

Jesus was born in Bethlehem—son of David and Son of God. The waiting for that is over. In the birth of Jesus, God kept His promise of old.

In the weeks ahead, we will commemorate that "coming"—we will retell it and rejoice in it—we will "celebrate Christmas"—because that part of what the world was waiting for it need wait for no longer. Our sins are paid for. Our future is secure—for all time. Our hearts are filled with the love and wisdom and power of God's Holy Spirit as a permanent presence. No one need wait on that anymore—no one who believes in Jesus.

But we Christians—followers of Christ—will also observe Advent—the season of anticipation—and preparation—for the coming of Christ—again. We wait, still, for the coming of our Lord Who came so many years ago, after so many years—centuries—of God's people—and the world—waiting.

---

[24] Luke 2:8-20.
[25] Luke 2:22-38.
[26] Luke 3:23.
[27] Luke 3:21-22.
[28] John 18:1-14.
[29] Luke 23:44-46.
[30] Matthew 28:1-6.

It was Jesus Himself Who promised that this part of the waiting would be worthwhile.

"Justice and righteousness—salvation and safety," the prophets had said. And they waited.

And Jesus came, and fulfilled the promise of God.

To us now, it doesn't seem so long to wait. We live in the present—*after* all that waiting. It was a harder wait for those who lived and died before His coming. They did not know when the waiting would be over.

Waiting for the return of our Lord as He promised is harder for us. The world today is much as Jesus described the warning signs then, and there is much to make people afraid in our day. The colorful accounts of cosmic chaos in the Bible take on a much more realistic tone in our technologically advanced times. We can do all the destructive things ourselves now, with remarkably little effort on the part of those who have access to great and demonic power.

But wait we must, because we cannot do otherwise. Still, we wait not for Armageddon,[31] or the Great Tribulation,[32] or any of the terrible things that could or might happen someday in this world gone sinfully wrong. We await our Lord's return—the Son of Man coming in a cloud with power and great glory, as He described it.

What are we waiting for?

The return of Christ, to us and for us, in the glorious conclusion of all that God has been doing to redeem this broken world. And knowing what we are waiting for tells us how we are to await it.

We are not waiting for a chance to get into a place where the best we can do is to race and wrestle with others for something that's not worth the effort—where there's not enough of whatever it is to go around anyway. Eternal peace and joy with God is not

---

[31] Revelation 16:16.
[32] Revelation 7:14.

some fleeting and over-hyped bargain. And it's not in limited supply. You don't have to beat somebody else out for your share. There is enough salvation to share with everybody.

We are not waiting for a bargain. The full price was paid, once and for all. It's a free gift for everybody who will accept it. There is no need for Anarchy, Bedlam or Chaos—and no benefit in dissipation, drunkenness or distress as we wait.

Unlike the Black Friday fanatics, we are not waiting for the doors to the stores to be opened. The doors into the Kingdom of Heaven are always open wide—and will remain open to all who will have faith in Christ—until He comes—without warning, apparently—and everything on earth is shut down for good and God moves everything—and everyone—He's saving to a new and better neighborhood forever.

We live our lives waiting—whether we realize it or not—for the most wonderful, remarkable thing that could ever be: the redemption of our infinitely loving, infinitely powerful God. The pain and the sorrow and the scary things in our lives and in our world that torment us will all disappear when what we await arrives. And when the waiting is over, we will stand before our Savior, straight and tall, with heads held high, to be welcomed by Him into the full and perfect experience of our never-ending relationship with Him.

Christmas is coming—and that's great.

But Christ is coming, too—and that's immeasurably greater.

Can't wait?

I understand how you feel, but you'll have to—we don't have a choice.

But oh, how "worth it" *this* wait will be!

5.

The Days Are Coming...

Jeremiah 33:14-16 NRSV

¹⁴ The days are surely coming, says the LORD, when I will fulfill the promise I made to the house of Israel and the house of Judah. ¹⁵ In those days and at that time I will cause a righteous Branch to spring up for David; and he shall execute justice and righteousness in the land. ¹⁶ In those days Judah will be saved and Jerusalem will live in safety. And this is the name by which it will be called: "The LORD is our righteousness."

☙◦❧

The world is a dangerous place. *We* may be living in the safest place on earth, but even we feel the anxiety of those who are at risk. We know that, even here, danger can reach us. There is no immunity from natural disaster or human depravity. We know what the world is like these days, and we worry about the days to come.

We should worry, if tomorrow is merely the mechanical outgrowth of today following the trajectory from yesterday. Even when we act with the best of intentions, the result is often disappointing. And far too many of our fellow "actors" in this world have no good intentions at all. Experience suggests that we should be worried about the future.

The Days Are Coming…

But, fortunately, the future is more than the accumulated momentum of the past. Tomorrow is more than the potluck stew cooked up with the random ingredients of today. There is another element to be considered that makes the future anything but mechanical.

"The days are…coming," says the Lord, *"when I will fulfill my promise."* The days are coming, says the Lord, when *"I will cause a righteous branch to spring up…and he shall execute justice and righteousness in the land."*

God engages us in the course of our lives and so God is engaged in human history. God is engaged as our lives move constantly out of our past, into the present, toward the future. Our future will not be simply-what-we-make-it. Our future will be our past—plus God.

"The days are coming," the prophet Jeremiah heard God say. "The future will not be what you think it's going to be," says God, "because I will be shaping it according to My divine plan and purpose."

How could Jeremiah write this? His world was falling apart. The leaders of his country were ignoring God and courting national disaster. Jeremiah challenged every false step, but his opposition to government policy only ensured his status as an enemy of the state—a security risk.

They did not appreciate his call for national repentance. They were incensed by his prophecies of doom. And then, as darkness fell over them—as violent death and destruction spread like a virus from town to town, consuming everything in its path—as all hope for the future was lost—God gave this same Jeremiah a message of hope—the promise of a special and glorious future—first spoken in the ancient past.

"I will fulfill the promise I made," says God. "I will do what I told David I would do for him: I will raise up a special descendent of his—long after he is dead and gone—to rule the world. I will do for My chosen people what I told them I would do for them. I will

enable this special descendent of David to execute justice and righteousness everywhere, to protect and preserve My people."³³

And so when Jeremiah's homeland was overrun by foreign powers and all that his people held dear was lost, they went into exile, knowing Jeremiah's condemnation had come to pass.

And throughout the many years of grief and heartache, they also held on to his words of hope: *"Days are coming,"* he had said. *"In those days, God will cause a righteous Branch to spring up."*

Their future was more than the sum of their past, because God had added hope to the mix. And the days came when God did fulfill His promise. The days came when God raised up a son of David, and this righteous Branch did bring justice and righteousness to all.

But God's promises are the sort that continue to be fulfilled. We live in the fulfillment of the hope promised through Jeremiah. The Righteous Branch has blessed every day of our past and brings justice and righteousness to us even now. But the days are coming, says the Lord, when He will fulfill His promise again—when the Righteous Branch will return in all His cosmic glory to bring an ultimate and final righteousness to this world.

Experience suggests that we should be worried about the future. God says we should not. The days of fulfillment are coming. God has raised up a Savior, as He promised. The Lord is our righteousness—and our future.

---

³³ 2 Samuel 7:1-17.

The Second Sunday in Advent

6.

Here He Comes

Matthew 3:1-3 ESV

¹ In those days John the Baptist came preaching in the wilderness of Judea, ² "Repent, for the kingdom of heaven is at hand." ³ For this is he who was spoken of by the prophet Isaiah when he said,
"The voice of one crying in the wilderness:
Prepare the way of the Lord;
make his paths straight.'"

☙❧

In the 1989 movie, *Field of Dreams*, a mysterious voice whispers to the main character, a California hippie turned Iowa farmer, "If you build it, he will come." So he builds "it." He builds a baseball field where his corn crop had been. And a famous baseball player from a bygone era does come. But his coming is not the end of the story. It's only the beginning. The farmer doesn't know it, but someone else is coming—someone much more important. The first man, as it turns out, is just setting the stage for that more important someone else.

...like John the Baptist did.

The place is Judea, not Iowa. And it's not a beautiful baseball field. It's a barren wilderness, of all things. But still, John the

Here He Comes

Baptist comes, as shoeless and colorful as the first ghostly ballplayer to appear on that Iowa farm field.

People come to see John the Baptist in the wilderness. But that is only the beginning of the story. Someone else is coming to that same Judean wilderness. Someone much more important than John the Baptist—famous as John has become. John is just setting the stage for the One Who is to come.

John comes with a message every bit as mysterious as the one that resulted in a ball field being built where the corn had been. But it's unlikely people heard his message in anything like the whisper of the movie. Instead, they heard: *"REPENT, FOR THE KINGDOM OF HEAVEN IS AT HAND!"* or to put it another way, "If you *repent*, He will come."

And that's what happened in the movie, in the end. The hippie turned farmer hears the voice that not everybody can hear. He responds in obedience to each message he hears. And through it all, he is reflecting on his life of rebellion against his father—and eventually, he repents the actions and attitudes that broke their relationship. In the end, the famous ball player points this Iowa farmer with the change of heart and mind to that more important someone else, who was right there on the field all along. The Iowa farmer is reconciled to his father who comes to him, not as he had known his father when he rebelled against him, but as a young man like himself.

In the movie, the farmer is asked about the field he built, "Is this heaven?"

He replies, "No, it's Iowa."

But he discovers that maybe heaven is as close as his front yard, not because Iowa is so heavenly, but because the kingdom of heaven is at hand.

That's what John the Baptist was preaching. And those who were willing to believe him discovered that it was true.

But why would people believe someone like John the Baptist? According to the scripture, John was a pretty wild guy, for his time.

Of course, he could wear his camel hair clothes from one end of the mall to the other today and nobody would notice. His grasshopper and honey lunch would fit right in with the sushi and tofu set. Today, if John the Baptist were to be branded as "weird," it would probably be for preaching in a public place without a pulpit or pews. And today, people would be shocked to be told they need to repent of anything.

Nevertheless, John came into the wilderness, preaching. John wasn't wasting his time...in the wilderness. You don't expect to find people in the wilderness, but there they are. There were people in the wilderness who listened to what John had to say. Some blew him off, but some took what he had to say to heart and acted accordingly. The Baptizer baptized them and then he pointed them to Someone much more important. They believed the good news—and entered the kingdom of heaven. People opened their hearts as John directed—and Jesus came.

When Jesus comes, God's kingdom comes with Him. Where Jesus goes, lives change—and the world changes. Always has; always will. Without Jesus, wherever you are is wilderness. The kingdom of heaven is the opposite of wilderness, but it surges into the wilderness like a determined rescue party, willing and able to reclaim the lost and dying for the kingdom.

The ultimate reality is that the kingdom of God is at hand, here for the taking. The proper response to this reality is repentance, turning to the kingdom represented in the person of Jesus Christ and embracing Him. Repent. Change your mind. Pick the kingdom instead of the wilderness.

That's what John the Baptist was preaching. And there ought to be a little bit of John the Baptist in every one of us Christians. These days you could come preaching in the wilderness of where you are. You don't have to be a weirdo to prepare the way for Jesus to come into the wilderness of other people's lives. John did not have spiritual impact because he was a colorful personality; his impact was the result of his letting God pack his life with the Holy

Spirit. John the Baptist went before Jesus to prepare the way for Him. And the Holy Spirit went before John to do the same for him.

Prepare: do something ahead of time. Pave the way for Jesus. Fill in the potholes. Clear away the obstacles. Make it easier for Jesus to get where He's going. And where is that? Jesus is headed straight for every human heart—yours and mine and his and hers. Jesus is coming anyway—whether we're ready or not.

If you want to prepare for the coming of Jesus the Messiah to His lost and helpless people, try speaking to people whose lives are empty, desolate, confused—wilderness. Pointing out the presence of God and His kingdom's availability, or encouraging people to look at their empty lives honestly and God's abundant love differently, can be done in a reasonable, normal tone of voice.

You don't have to do the "John the Baptist thing." But if you don't, it will be harder for the message of salvation to get through the crooked and cluttered lives of those who live those lives in a modern, materially-obsessed wilderness. What's the chance that someone will repent if he doesn't know that the kingdom of God is at hand.

People can get into the "Christmas spirit" (or as we have been taught to say these days: "the non-faith-specific, spiritually-sanitized, commercially-saturated, emotionally-intensified, early-winter holiday experience"), without Christ getting into them.

But Jesus did come. And Jesus is coming again. The kingdom of God is at hand.

As John the Baptist would say, "Let's get out there and make some noise."

The Second Sunday in Advent

2 Peter 3:8-15b NRSV

⁸ But do not ignore this one fact, beloved, that with the Lord one day is like a thousand years, and a thousand years are like one day. ⁹ The Lord is not slow about his promise, as some think of slowness, but is patient with you, not wanting any to perish, but all to come to repentance. ¹⁰ But the day of the Lord will come like a thief, and then the heavens will pass away with a loud noise, and the elements will be dissolved with fire, and the earth and everything that is done on it will be disclosed.

¹¹ Since all these things are to be dissolved in this way, what sort of persons ought you to be in leading lives of holiness and godliness, ¹² waiting for and hastening the coming of the day of God, because of which the heavens will be set ablaze and dissolved, and the elements will melt with fire? ¹³ But, in accordance with his promise, we wait for new heavens and a new earth, where righteousness is at home.

¹⁴ Therefore, beloved, while you are waiting for these things, strive to be found by him at peace, without spot or blemish; ¹⁵ and regard the patience of our Lord as salvation.

7.

Patient Salvation

2 Peter 3:8-15b NRSV

How long is long enough?
How long is too long?
How long should we wait?
And should we wait at all?

They were asking these questions before the ink was dry on the New Testament: How long should we wait for Jesus to come back? Should we wait at all?

And here we are two thousand years later and—Can you believe it?—we're still asking the same questions—because we're still waiting—still waiting for Jesus to come back. He said He would, but He hasn't yet. How long should we wait?

Some decided, before the ink was dry, that we shouldn't wait at all. If He hadn't come, He wouldn't come. With each day, each year, each lifetime, more decided we should not wait. If He could come—if He was going to come—He would have come, surely, by now. If you were Jesus, and you told everybody you were coming back, wouldn't you have done so by now?

"If He hasn't come by now, He isn't coming."

How do you figure that?

Patient Salvation

"Well, if Jesus hasn't returned, it isn't very likely that there is a God, at least a God Who calls Jesus His only Begotten Son. Or put the other way around: if there is no God, Jesus is not very likely to return, since His return is heavily dependent on there being a God willing and able to send Him."[34]

It has a certain logic to it—this argument from absence. And it's certainly an attractive viewpoint for those who desire to live unconstrained by any concern about the return of a morally-minded Messiah. As C.S. Lewis recognized, "If there is no God, all things are permissible."[35] "Anything goes" because He's not coming—to stop it or punish it.

But what seems logical is not always provable—and may certainly not be right. What you would do if you were Jesus is totally irrelevant, of course, because you're not Jesus. If there is no God, there's no one to wait for.

But if there is a God, you might want to wait a bit longer. If there is a God, there is also a reason Jesus has not come back yet.

Why hasn't God sent Jesus back as Jesus promised? Is God lazy? Not likely: He *"created the heavens and the earth"* and *"all that dwell therein."*[36] Is God indifferent? He *"so loved the world that he gave his only begotten Son."*[37] Is God powerless? He raised Jesus from the dead and defeated death in the process.[38]

So what's going on? Why are we still waiting, after all these years?

Maybe it's a gift. Maybe God is giving what only He can give: time. When Jesus comes back, the gig is up. The show is over. Time is up in the ultimate, cosmic sense, for everybody. But until He

---

[34] 1 Corinthians 15:12-19.
[35] This is the argument he makes in *Mere Christianity*, though the idea is presented even earlier in Fyodor Dostoevsky's *The Brothers Karamazov*. Those listening to the sermon would have been more familiar with C. S. Lewis.
[36] Genesis 1, KJV; Psalm 24:1, KJV.
[37] John 3:16, KJV.
[38] Romans 8:11.

comes, there is time to be saved, time enough to avoid a destruction that is otherwise certain.

It's like a "divine Dunkirk." In May of 1940, an army of British soldiers was defeated, defenseless, and waiting to be destroyed. But certain death did not come. The day of reckoning was miraculously delayed just long enough for multitudes to be rescued, to be carried across to safety on the other side.

Until Jesus, the righteous Judge, returns, there is time for the doomed to be rescued—which, of course, is what Jesus, Who has not yet come, and His heavenly Father, Who does not desire that any should perish, have in mind.

Powerlessness? No, patience. Long-delayed? Not from the perspective of an eternal God. How long should we wait? How long should He wait, if delay is deliverance? He's not dawdling, you know. He's delaying—for the sake of salvation.

And Along Came John

Malachi 3:1-3; 4:5-6 ESV

3¹ *"Behold, I send my messenger, and he will prepare the way before me. And the Lord whom you seek will suddenly come to his temple; and the messenger of the covenant in whom you delight, behold, he is coming, says the Lord of hosts. ² But who can endure the day of his coming, and who can stand when he appears? For he is like a refiner's fire and like fullers' soap. ³ He will sit as a refiner and purifier of silver, and he will purify the sons of Levi and refine them like gold and silver, and they will bring offerings in righteousness to the Lord."*

4⁵ *"Behold, I will send you Elijah the prophet before the great and awesome day of the Lord comes. ⁶ And he will turn the hearts of fathers to their children and the hearts of children to their fathers, lest I come and strike the land with a decree of utter destruction."*

The Second Sunday in Advent

Luke 1:5-25 ESV

⁵ *In the days of Herod, king of Judea, there was a priest named Zechariah, of the division of Abijah. And he had a wife from the daughters of Aaron, and her name was Elizabeth.* ⁶ *And they were both righteous before God, walking blamelessly in all the commandments and statutes of the Lord.* ⁷ *But they had no child, because Elizabeth was barren, and both were advanced in years.*

⁸ *Now while he was serving as priest before God when his division was on duty,* ⁹ *according to the custom of the priesthood, he was chosen by lot to enter the temple of the Lord and burn incense.* ¹⁰ *And the whole multitude of the people were praying outside at the hour of incense.* ¹¹ *And there appeared to him an angel of the Lord standing on the right side of the altar of incense.* ¹² *And Zechariah was troubled when he saw him, and fear fell upon him.* ¹³ *But the angel said to him, "Do not be afraid, Zechariah, for your prayer has been heard, and your wife Elizabeth will bear you a son, and you shall call his name John.* ¹⁴ *And you will have joy and gladness, and many will rejoice at his birth,* ¹⁵ *for he will be great before the Lord. And he must not drink wine or strong drink, and he will be filled with the Holy Spirit, even from his mother's womb.* ¹⁶ *And he will turn many of the children of Israel to the Lord their God,* ¹⁷ *and he will go before him in the spirit and power of Elijah, to turn the hearts of the fathers to the children, and the disobedient to the wisdom of the just, to make ready for the Lord a people prepared."*

¹⁸ *And Zechariah said to the angel, "How shall I know this? For I am an old man, and my wife is advanced in years."* ¹⁹ *And the angel answered him, "I am Gabriel. I stand in the presence of God, and I was sent to speak to you and to bring you this good news.* ²⁰ *And behold, you will be silent and unable to speak until the day that these things take place, because you did not believe my words, which will be fulfilled in their time."* ²¹ *And the people were waiting for Zechariah, and they were wondering at his delay in the temple.* ²² *And when he came out, he was unable to speak to them, and they realized that he had seen a vision in the temple. And he kept making signs to them and remained mute.* ²³ *And when his time of service was ended, he went to his home.*

24 After these days his wife Elizabeth conceived, and for five months she kept herself hidden, saying, *25* "Thus the Lord has done for me in the days when he looked on me, to take away my reproach among people."

ತಿ⊷⊚

8.

And Along Came John

Malachi 3:1-3 and 4:5-6; Luke 1:5-25 ESV

"Behold, I will send my messenger...!"
"Behold, I will send you Elijah...!"
And then—nothing.

God spoke one last majestic word of promise through the prophet Malachi—and then: silence—for years and years and centuries. A word of God, full of hope, and at the same time, full of dreadful judgment for those on the wrong side of it.

All the story of the Bible, from Creation[39] through Abraham and Sarah and the birth of Isaac[40]—from the birth of Samuel to a barren Hannah[41] and the choice of David to rule a chosen people[42]—from Moses leading those people out of captivity[43] and their own disobedience driving them back into it (according to the powerful message of many prophets) until, finally, God's last word, seemingly, left His people waiting—hanging—anticipating something else—some-*one* else.

---

[39] Genesis 1—2.
[40] Genesis 12—21.
[41] 1 Samuel 1.
[42] 1 Samuel 16.
[43] Exodus 3—15.

And so for centuries, God's people go on about their lives—waiting, hoping, wondering—wondering when God would fulfill this last promise and send His messenger. Generation after generation, appearing and living and dying, all waiting for Elijah to appear—the mighty prophet Elijah,[44] the announcer of droughts, the challenger of kings, the slayer of idolaters and the raiser of the dead—the caller down of fire upon altars and the rider of fiery chariots to heaven. *"Behold, I will send you Elijah!"*

And yet, after a while—after a lifetime—you get used to the silence and don't expect to hear anything else. You don't expect to see the angel that Daniel saw—the archangel Gabriel.[45] You don't really expect anything as you go about your business, doing the best you can with what your life has become.

Even if you're a priest—a servant of this God Who hasn't spoken a new word in many lifetimes—you go about your business—you do your duty, as Luke says, lighting the incense to God on His altar in His Temple, looking for nothing out of the ordinary because you've never seen anything out of the ordinary. You do your duty so the people waiting outside can at least get their priest's blessing as they go on waiting for the messenger God has promised—the Elijah He said He would sent.

And then one day, without warning—except for the warning of Malachi left hanging out there for so long—you go about your business as usual and the most unusual thing in the world happens. An old priest named Zechariah is doing his duty like he's always done—like everyone else does. Zechariah goes into the Holy Place in the Temple to worship God and he discovers that this time, he is not alone. Not that he ever was, really, though it always seemed that way.

But this time, there's no doubt. This time, there's an angel—an *arch*-angel!—standing where the old priest normally goes about his business as usual.

---

[44] 1 Kings 17—2 Kings 2.
[45] Daniel 7.

Seeing an angel can take your breath away. Before the conversation is over, the angel will take the old man's voice away, too.

Funny, isn't it? Zechariah has more to say now than he ever had in his whole life, and he can't say a word. On the other hand, his inability to speak speaks volumes. That long-ago last word of God is superseded by a new word of God, fulfilling it. It is a word of divine promise—of personal and spiritual hope satisfied. A man grown old will finally become a father. And a people grown old and tired spiritually will come to life again. The messenger of the Lord—the Elijah-like prophet—is on his way, and even more amazing things are going to start happening when he comes. God's Elijah is finally coming—and his name will be "John."

And what will he do?

He will point out the spiritual problems of God's people, and then he will point God's people to the One Who is the fulfillment of all God's promises. We have not yet started to talk about the birth of Jesus or His miraculous conception or even the announcement of His coming, and already, God is preparing for the salvation that is to come through Him. God is preparing for the salvation of Jesus by sending a messenger before Him: John.

There is only one Jesus, and it sounded as though there would only be one John. But, in fact, there turned out to be countless Johns, forerunners of the Messiah, messengers of God who pointed others to the Christ Who came after them. When John comes along, Jesus will not be far behind.

What did the archangel say about John? He will be filled with the Holy Spirit. He will be great before the Lord. He will go before Him in the spirit and power of Elijah. He will be an answer to prayer. Many people will rejoice at his birth because he will turn many to their God, to make them ready for the Lord.

Now get this: for hundreds of years, people had been reading Malachi and expecting Elijah to come along some day. And then one day, Gabriel turns up in the Temple and tells the priest on duty that day that Elijah is coming along, except that when he does come along, you're going to know him as John (the Baptist).

Now suppose that today, as you're listening to Gabriel talk about John the Baptist coming along, John does come along, but John turns out to be *you*.

Somebody was John for you. Somebody told you about Jesus—confronted you about your sins and called on you to repent and pointed you to the Lord. That somebody, like John, was filled with the Holy Spirit and was great before the Lord—great enough to get you focused and moving in the right direction. Somebody was an answer to your prayer, even if you didn't know you needed to be praying it. Somebody got you ready for the Lord—and aren't you glad?

So...

"But *I'm* no John the Baptist! *I'm* no Elijah!"

Oh really? How do you know Gabriel isn't speaking to somebody, somewhere, right now, promising them a messenger from the Lord: you?

"*I* can't go anywhere in the spirit and power of Elijah!" And Elizabeth was too old to give birth to a baby, who, according to the Gospel, was born about nine months after the angel appeared and announced it.

"I wouldn't know what to say!"

Zechariah couldn't say anything until he said the one word the angel gave him to say: "John."

Look in the mirror when you go home. You won't see some wild-eyed wilderness wanderer in a camel skin cape covered with insects and honey—I don't think. But what you will see is a messenger of the Lord—a John or Jane the Baptist whom the Holy Spirit will empower to turn hearts back to God like wayward children to their loving parents.

You want to prepare for Christmas? Forget the trees and the lights and the baubles for a bit and focus on being the messenger the Lord will send before the Savior.

The Second Sunday in Advent

Tis the season to come along—like John—in the power and spirit of Elijah.

Luke 3:1-6 NRSV

¹ *In the fifteenth year of the reign of Tiberius Caesar, Pontius Pilate being governor of Judea, and Herod being tetrarch of Galilee, and his brother Philip tetrarch of the region of Ituraea and Trachonitis, and Lysanias tetrarch of Abilene,* ² *during the high priesthood of Annas and Caiaphas, the word of God came to John the son of Zechariah in the wilderness.* ³ *And he went into all the region around the Jordan, proclaiming a baptism of repentance for the forgiveness of sins.* ⁴ *As it is written in the book of the words of Isaiah the prophet,*

> *"The voice of one crying in the wilderness:*
> *'Prepare the way of the Lord,*
>   *make his paths straight.*
> ⁵ *Every valley shall be filled,*
>   *and every mountain and hill shall be made low,*
>   *and the crooked shall become straight,*
>   *and the rough places shall become level ways,*
> ⁶ *and all flesh shall see the salvation of God.'"*

9.

God's Advance Man

Luke 3:1-6 NRSV

Luke's introduction to the gospel proper sounds like the guest list for some big state dinner: the Roman emperor, the governor of Judea, assorted petty potentates, the big dogs of the religious establishment—and John Zachariahson.

"Wait a minute! How did *he* sneak in here? He's *nobody*!"

Maybe not, but he's going to get all the attention.

However, before we attend to John, let's notice what Luke is *not* saying. If the word of God came to John *"in the fifteenth year of the reign of Emperor Tiberius, when Pontius Pilate was governor of Judea, and Herod was ruler of Galilee, and his brother Philip was the ruler of Ituraea and Trachonitis, and Lysanias was the ruler of Abilene, during the highpriesthood of Annas and Caiaphas,"* then the word of God did *not* come to Tiberius in his imperial capital, or to Pilate in his governor's palace, or to Herod or Philip or Lysanius in their sumptuous chalets scattered across the countryside—or to Annas or his son-in-law, Caiaphas, running the Jewish religion in the remarkable Jerusalem Temple.

In the story about to unfold, all of these supposedly heavy hitters turn out to be bit players. Some will come back—briefly—at the end of the story. But contrary to their press clippings, they really don't matter in the only story that does. While all these guys were thinking, and acting like, and being treated like they were important, the word of God came to a guy named John, a Jewish nobody who never sat on a royal throne or walked the corridors of religious or political power.

This John wandered around in the wilderness of a puny province on the outer edge of the empire. Out there in the wilderness, the word of God came to John, just like it came centuries before to guys like Hosea and Micah—and Jeremiah and Joel and Jonah.

To say "the word of God came to" someone is to say that person is a prophet. And Luke says, *"...the word of God came to John."*

Of course, the word of God doesn't just come *to* a prophet—it comes *upon* him, or *over* him. The word of God is a power that takes control of a prophet. The word of God came to—or upon—John, and as a result, John went to God's people and prophesied—he gave them a message from God.

What did John say?

"Repent and show you mean it by being baptized so that you will be qualified by your repentance to have your sins forgiven."

According to Luke, the message is not new; John is just repeating what the prophet Isaiah said almost 600 years earlier:

"Prepare the way of the Lord;
make his paths straight."

...which means that God is still saying and meaning what He meant back then, and from the beginning—and what He has meant ever since.

You see, even though John is far more important than all these very important men in the world of his day, there is One Who is infinitely more important even than John. That infinitely more important One is coming, but first, John is directed to prepare the way for Him. For all his importance—for all his spiritual significance as a genuine prophet (and the last prophet in the Old Testament mold)—John is actually an "advance man," someone who is sent ahead to get everything ready for the arrival of Another Who is far more important.

The One Who is coming is God Himself. "Prepare for His coming," says John. "Repair the road."

Before there were highway departments and contractors, the responsibility for maintaining roads fell to the population at large. People were responsible for repairing the section of road that ran by or to their homes.

In those times, it was also common for rulers to tour their realms to see and be seen by their subjects. And wherever a ruler went, riders were sent ahead to inform the people that their king was coming. Preparations were to be made to receive him properly.

Foremost among the preparations was putting the roads the king would travel on in order. Ancient roads were often pitted and overgrown. Some were all but impassable, especially if they had been neglected. But the king was coming, and they had to prepare his way.

Our King is coming and He is no petty potentate. He is the King of kings and Lord of lords. And the messenger has been sent with a message:

"Prepare the way.
Prepare the way of the Lord.
Make his paths straight."

God is coming to you. He is coming to your heart and your life. But it is His way and His path. When He created you, God created a way for Him to enter your life. He created a path straight to your heart. God's intention and desire has always been to come to you and share your life with you—to fill your heart with His love and grace and glory.

But pride and bitterness push up barriers on His path to you. Despair digs holes in the way. Selfishness and deceit make crooked the way He created straight. Sins large and small soon turn the smooth path rough.

So how do you repair the spiritual road—God's road to your heart?

According to John—which means according to God—repentance repairs and prepares the way of the Lord. Turning from sin straightens out the crooked path. Genuine repentance restores the proper foundation for receiving God's forgiveness, the royal gift of grace.

Isaiah said,

> *"Every valley shall be raised up,*
> *every mountain and hill made low;*
> *the rough ground shall become level,*
> *the rugged places a plain."*[46]

All this shall be done. But all that is required of you—all that God demands—is repentance. The rest, He will do—for you and in you.

But there's one more thing: when the King returns, *"all flesh shall see the salvation of God."*

If you repent of your sins and prepare the way for His coming to you, you will see His salvation within you as you accept it and experience it.

If you ignore the word of God—if you avoid or neglect the preparation of repentance God directs—you will also see His salvation one day. You will see it as that lost hope you do not have and would now give anything and everything to possess.

The word of God came to John as it came to the Old Testament prophets—and as it would come to the first disciples of Jesus after His Resurrection—and then to all those who have believed in Jesus in all the years since. It has come to us who now believe and have repented and have been forgiven.

Now, *we* are John. Now *we* are the advance men and women for the One Who has come—and will come again.

"Oh, but *I'm* no John the Baptist!"

---

[46] Isaiah 40:4, NIV.

Well, you're in luck. Today, there's no requirement to live in the wild or eat weird stuff or dress like a wacko. But Jesus is coming back, and He's told us to go before Him and tell the world to get ready.

Yes, the idea of doing that is a bit daunting. But it wasn't easy for John, either. He probably amused some people—he certainly offended quite a few others. No doubt, he terrified some who thought he was out of his mind.

But there were people who heard him and got the message and repented and prepared the way and saw the salvation of God settle into their hearts when they met Jesus face to face.

The word of God came to John. The word of God has come to you. What are you going to do with it while you await His coming?

The Third Sunday in Advent

Is Jesus the One?

Matthew 11:2-11 ESV

² Now when John heard in prison about the deeds of the Christ, he sent word by his disciples ³ and said to [Jesus], "Are you the one who is to come, or shall we look for another?" ⁴ And Jesus answered them, "Go and tell John what you hear and see: ⁵ the blind receive their sight and the lame walk, lepers are cleansed and the deaf hear, and the dead are raised up, and the poor have good news preached to them. ⁶ And blessed is the one who is not offended by me."

⁷ As they went away, Jesus began to speak to the crowds concerning John: "What did you go out into the wilderness to see? A reed shaken by the wind? ⁸ What then did you go out to see? A man dressed in soft clothing? Behold, those who wear soft clothing are in kings' houses. ⁹ What then did you go out to see? A prophet? Yes, I tell you, and more than a prophet. ¹⁰ This is he of whom it is written,

> 'Behold, I send my messenger before your face,
> who will prepare your way before you.'

¹¹ "Truly, I say to you, among those born of women there has arisen no one greater than John the Baptist. Yet the one who is least in the kingdom of heaven is greater than he."

10.

Is Jesus the One?

Matthew 11:2-11 ESV

It is such a delight to see the Nativity scenes going up in so many places around town, including the one on our corner. But the scene in the gospel today bears none of the beauty of the Christmas that is coming. The Bible paints a somber scene, far removed from the business in Bethlehem.

Matthew takes us first to a place that is dark and cold—where fear and misery vie for the upper hand in the minds of a small multitude held there against their will. Welcome to King Herod's dungeon and the pathetic people chained inside, one of whom is of particular interest to us this morning—a fellow called John the Baptist.

John the Baptist was a powerful presence in the wilderness—calling people out of their sins—calling them to repentance—wiping out their useless excuses and warning them of the fiery judgment to come. Not a nice word for anybody—and yet, they came out into the barren wasteland in droves to hear him.

John didn't have the word "compliment" in his vocabulary—until the day Jesus came along with all the rest and got in line at the river and received at the hand of John the baptism John knew himself unworthy to perform.

When Jesus first came out to John, the prophet of doom became the prophet of hope: "There He is!" John said the day Jesus showed up. In fact, even before Jesus got there, John was pointing Him out to the crowd: "Look! Here comes the Lamb of God Who takes away the sin of the world!" Whoa! That's high praise indeed from someone who puts everybody else in the "brood of vipers" category.

Even before Jesus got there, John was pointing Jesus out to people who needed to know Him—who needed to turn away from everything else and follow Him.

And that's why, amid all the characters of Christmas—the glorious angels and majestic wise men—the humble shepherds and the holy family—this wild man John the Baptist shows up in the run up to the coming of Christ.

You light the Christmas candles and listen to the comforting carols—and then John jumps into the picture and shouts, "Here He comes! Don't forget in all the decorating, shopping and festivities: Jesus is coming." Jesus—holy Child, Babe in a manger—yes. But Lamb of God, Savior of the world, Suffering Messiah, Risen Lord, as well.

John the Baptist was a prophet in the "old school" Old Testament tradition like Elijah and Jeremiah. Everybody could see that.[47] But Jesus said that John was more than that—more than Moses or Isaiah. Jesus spoke about John the Baptist to the crowd gathered around Him and called John an Advent messenger. John is the one God sent to prepare the way of the Messiah. John was God's messenger to get people ready to see Jesus. That's John the Baptist in the wilderness, doing his "Prepare ye the way!" stuff.

Now here—at this point in the sermon—I would normally make the transition to practical application and point out to you that you, too, are to be God's messengers, foretelling the coming of Christ. You, like John, are to be preparing the way of the

---

[47] Matthew 16:13-14.

Messiah—in your own hearts and lives, of course, as a matter of Christian devotion.

But you are also to be the John the Baptism figure to others. Maybe not yelling out their sins at the traffic circles or pointing the finger of judgment at them as they wander around the Wal-Mart. But surely you can speak quietly of Jesus in grocery store conversations or gently point to Jesus at a holiday get-together when someone points to an emptiness inside. John the Baptist was the messenger God sent to prepare the way for Jesus in this world—in normal, everyday people—and so are we.

But imagine the emotional and psychological impact of being cooped up and languishing in a prison cell on a "wide-open-spaces" guy like John. It's bad enough to imprison the body; it's far worse to imprison the soul.

And John was a fellow who lived his life and served his God "wide-open." Now John sits in a stone box, awaiting the worst.

But even in prison, you can hear about Jesus and what He's doing. Even in prison, the soul can be set free.

Having heard, in prison, about what Jesus was doing, John the Baptist sent some of his followers to quiz Jesus about it: "I'm hearing about what you're doing. What does it mean? Are You the One?" John asked from his prison cell. "Is it You or someone else?"

And Jesus also spoke to John—through the men John sent to question Him. Jesus said to them, "Tell John what you see. Tell him what's going on. And tell him this, too: *Blessed is the man who does not fall away on account of me."* Now, *there's* a verse you don't see written on a lot of Christmas cards!

But it points up a fact we ought to face. Not all of us come to Christmas with joy in our hearts and spring in our steps.

As wonderful as the idea of Christmas is, your experience may share a little—or a lot—with John the Baptist, who is stuck in a terrible situation and left wondering what he can trust about everything he's believed in.

It's hard to embrace the joy of Christmas when you're locked up in miserable or scary circumstances. You don't have to be in prison, of course; poor health will do. So will the loss of a loved one—or a job—conflict within your family—children or grandchildren who have lost their way, morally or spiritually—any pain or sorrow or difficulty.

"Merry Christmas?"

You wish!

But you're a Christian! It's the birth of the Savior! The Christ Child is coming! Yes, you hear all the wonderful things that you yourself have told others in the past. But this year, it's different. You hear all the wonderful things, but your heart is held captive by something that makes Christmas the last thing on your mind.

And if that's not the case this year, your turn with John's suffering and uncertainty will likely come, someday, just like Christmases do.

"Why am I having to go through this? What have I done to deserve this? What's the point of believing in Jesus if this is what I have to go through?" The hard things in our lives make it hard to get in "the Christmas spirit"—as hard as it was for John the Baptist, locked in his cell.

But John didn't suffer in silence. He sent word to Jesus. "I hear what you're doing, Jesus, but I'm not seeing much of it in my life. Are You 'the One'? Are You God's answer to my problems? Are You coming to help me? Is Christmas going to make any difference for me? Are You the One Who is to come, or should I be looking somewhere else? Should I be looking for somebody else?"

John the Baptist "need[s] a little Christmas, right this very minute," as the song goes.[48]

And, remember: this guy, according to Jesus, is the greatest guy God ever put on earth—except for Jesus. Isn't it amazing what

---

[48] From "We Need a Little Christmas," Jerry Herman, composer (for the Broadway musical, *Mame*), 1966.

adversity can do to your frame of mind—and your faith—even if you're John the Baptist?

So if you're finding the Christmas season a little difficult this year—if you're having a little trouble getting in the swing of things because Jesus seems just a little too far away from what you're going through—listen to what Jesus tells John: *"The blind see, the lame walk, the sick are cured, the deaf hear, the dead are raised, and the gospel is preached to the poor."*

"Just like you told them, John, the Lamb of God has come and God is changing the world through Him. John, you are suffering, but Christmas has come to the world, and the Christ Who was born in Bethlehem has grown up and into the job God sent Him here to do—just like you said He would. What you're going through right now doesn't change the fact that what you've always believed—what you've always looked for and hoped for—is happening just the way God intended."

Jesus doesn't answer John's question, except to list the kinds of miracles that are taking place every day—and to offer an odd blessing: *"Blessed is the man,"* Jesus says, *"who does not fall away on account of me."*

You've believed faithfully and acted courageously in doing the task God has given you. You've helped to unleash the power of Christmas on a lost and needy world. But right now, there's not a lot of the sense of the miracle of Christmas in *your* life. And to the wide-open John whose life is now locked down—and to anyone having the "John-in-captivity" experience—Jesus sends word through His Word, and through all that we do to prepare for and celebrate Christmas: "Do not lose heart—do not despair—do not doubt that God is doing what He intended to do in sending Jesus into this world."

You see, just as the Christ Child came at Christmas as a Baby born into this world, Christ Jesus will come back to this world in glory.

He will return, not as a helpless, holy Child, but as the cosmic Lord and everlasting King, and all the sorrows and sufferings of Christmases past will be wiped away in an instant for every Christian.

"John, blessed are you there in that prison, if you do not lose heart." And blessed are all of you who think that Christmas will not be what it ought to be for you this year, but still listen to Jesus and trust in Jesus and ask Jesus the hard questions, and still do not fall away because of what you're going through right now. Blessed are you who have decided that Jesus is the One Who is to come, regardless of anything else.

Jesus is the One and He is coming. He is coming at Christmas and He is coming to you. Believe that—whatever your circumstances—and you'll end up greater than John the Baptist—according to Jesus—because you'll be celebrating Christmas as part of the kingdom of God.

Merry Christmas—for sure!

11.

Restore Our Fortunes

Psalm 126 ESV

*¹ When the Lord restored the fortunes of Zion,
    we were like those who dream.
² Then our mouth was filled with laughter,
    and our tongue with shouts of joy;
then they said among the nations,
    "The Lord has done great things for them."
³ The Lord has done great things for us;
    we are glad.
⁴ Restore our fortunes, O Lord,
    like streams in the Negeb!
⁵ Those who sow in tears
    shall reap with shouts of joy!
⁶ He who goes out weeping,
    bearing the seed for sowing,
shall come home with shouts of joy,
    bringing his sheaves with him.*

※

    Have any of you considered how remarkable it is that we would be provided a psalm to recite today that is really a prayer that God would restore our fortunes? The lectionary assigning this psalm to this day was published in 1992. That's a long time ago! Now I ask you: How did they know?[49]

"*Restore our fortunes, O Lord—like streams in the Negev.*" Except that there aren't any streams in the Negev—usually. The Negev is the desert that stretches across the southern part of Israel and, most of the time, there's no water there. The streambeds are dry.

But if the rains come—if a storm breaks over the desert—the Negev is transformed, and water flows everywhere, and the desert comes to life. It is immediate. It is massive. It is miraculous. "Restore our fortunes, O Lord, like rivers in the desert."

ಶ್ರೀ

Just about everybody has lost a fortune of some size or other this year. Those big old nest eggs they used to show everybody carrying around in those investment commercials will probably all fit back in the little egg cartons now. We've talked a lot in our sermons about what we've all lost over the past few months, but this time—this morning—in this passage, it's not about the money. Really.

The fortunes the people of God are praying for are not financial. They're praying about their fate, their destiny, the experiences of their lives as a people that form their identity. When we pray their words, their prayer, we're praying for things far more important than an "up-tick" in the stock market—as nice as that would be. We're praying about the meaning and purpose of our lives, about our relationship with God in this world and the next.

You survived the geography lesson a minute ago. Let's see how you do with a little history.

The psalm begins with the memory of God bringing captives back to Zion, the hill in Jerusalem where the Temple of Solomon was built. The captives in the psalm were the Jewish people taken

---

[49] This sermon was preached in 2008, during the economic downturn, to many who were depending on investments for retirement income.

away to Babylon when their country was conquered and their capital destroyed.⁵⁰ And in Babylon they stayed, exiles held captive, for 70 years.⁵¹

But nations rise and nations fall, and God restores the fortunes of His people. The great Babylon was conquered as little Judah had been. The Jewish people were released from their captivity and allowed to go home. And those who did, entered Jerusalem and climbed Mount Zion in a state of euphoria. The Lord had brought them back to Zion. Against all odds, defying all logic, God had brought them back. The Lord had restored their fortunes.

But not their portfolios. It's ironic: many of the Jews had made a lot of money in Babylon—as exiles. Many of them chose to stay there—with their money and the businesses that made the money.

On the other hand, many of the Jews who undertook the journey back to Jerusalem had little money. And there was even less to be made once they got there.

But they were in Jerusalem—they had returned to Zion out of captivity—and they understood that their fortunes had been restored. They were again in their lives where God wanted them to be and who God wanted them to be and they knew that God alone had made it happen.

And the knowledge that God had restored their fortunes left them stunned. How could they have been released from their lifetime of bondage? How could they be standing on holy ground? How could they be so fortunate—so blessed?

Sometimes you experience something so wonderful that you simply can't explain it. If you try to explain it, it just leaves you speechless—like someone in a trance—dreaming. I've seen that look on the face of little children the instant they see all the presents on Christmas morning.

But what you can't explain, you can celebrate. And when you start to celebrate, the laughter comes. When the Lord brought back

---

⁵⁰ Jeremiah 52.
⁵¹ Jeremiah 29:10.

the captives to Zion, first they were like men who dreamed—and then their mouths were filled with laughter.

Do you get the picture? Not pleasant smiles or friendly chuckles, but laughter you can't hold back—laughter that spreads your lips so wide that your face almost disappears.

And the joy! You know, you can have so much joy in your heart that it spreads to your tongue and makes you want to sing so bad that you don't care if you don't know one note from another and couldn't hit the right pitch with a pitch pipe—or a pitching wedge, for that matter.

And people could tell something had happened to them. Even people who didn't particularly like them had to admit, based on what they saw, "The Lord has done great things for them." You couldn't miss it.

But if you weren't one of the captives God set free, you didn't know the half of it. Nobody knows what it's like to have your fortunes restored by God unless it's happened to you.

And maybe no one knows what it's like to need your fortunes restored by God unless He's restored your fortunes before. God broke the bonds of their captivity. He brought them back to Zion. He gave them something miraculous to celebrate.

But life wasn't all eggnog and mistletoe—even then. Even life in the Holy Land can be hard. Life as the people of God was a constant struggle with everybody else. The people of God didn't always get along with each other, either. And then times got hard. So they prayed.

"Restore our fortunes, O Lord. Life has become so dry and barren. We remember what You did when You brought us to this place. We remember when You set us free. We know You had a divine purpose in that, but that purpose is not yet fulfilled."

"Restore our fortunes," they pray. "Shower us with Your life-giving power and fulfill Your purpose in redeeming us."

And what does the Lord say?

The Third Sunday in Advent

"Those who sow in tears will reap with songs of joy." Not exactly what you want to hear when you're praying for your basic fortune restoration. You pray a prayer like that and you want to hear something like, "Coming right up!" or "Let the good times roll!" or at least, "Let me think about it and I'll get back to you." Instead, it's "Sow in tears…reap with joy."

Even when God restores the fortunes of His people—even when He takes them out of bondage and returns them from exile—even when God saves people—He sets them in a hard place where they have a job to do. God sets His people in His field, to plant seed in stubborn soil. The work is hard because the soil is so often unyielding. And the sower weeps, knowing that not every seed, precious as it is, will bear fruit.

But the sacrifice and sorrow involved in sowing seed is not God's final answer. The present sacrifice, offered by the people of God in memory of His first great work to restore their fortunes, is also offered in hope of the great work that is to come—the joyful harvest.

They prayed about Babylon and Zion, conquest and captivity and coming back to the land of promise. And when we, as Christians, pray for the restoration of our fortunes, what are we praying for? We have not been held prisoner in Babylon or released to the land of our ancestors. Our captivity has been to sin and our coming back is to the bosom of God the Father. Our eternal fortunes were restored when a Child born in holiness and humility grew to manhood and died in sacrificial agony as God intended.

And in that holy Child—that special Man—God broke the bonds of our captivity to sin and death. He brought us back to the Zion of His heart. He gave us something miraculous to celebrate. And so we laugh for joy and sing at the birth of our Messiah.

But the life of the Christian is still hard. We await the fulfillment of the promise of redemption amid the frustration of a world still given over to sin and death.

And rather than relishing our eternal reward in heaven, we remain rooted in this world, struggling to sow the seeds of the gospel, weeping over all that undermines our success, in the world, and in us.

We have known the restoration of our fortunes in the grace of our God. We celebrate Christmas with wonder, laughter and song. We know, even now, the hardships of life in the Lord, even at Christmas time. We sow each day the seeds of salvation, weeping to see the world in its fallen-ness around us, weeping to see the opposition it raises to our word.

But we await the final restoration of our fortunes as Christians, when the weeping of the present—the sorrows and sacrifices of each day—will give way to the joyful song of heaven's harvest, and the Christ Who came…will come again.

> *"When the Lord restored the fortunes of Zion,*
> *we were like those who dream.*
> *Then our mouth was filled with laughter,*
> *and our tongues with shouts of joy."*

Restore our fortunes again, O Lord. Restore our fortunes again.

Zephaniah 3:14-20 RSV

¹⁴ Sing aloud, O daughter of Zion;
  shout, O Israel!
Rejoice and exult with all your heart,
  O daughter of Jerusalem!
¹⁵ The LORD has taken away the judgments against you,
  he has cast out your enemies.
The King of Israel, the LORD, is in your midst;
  you shall fear evil no more.
¹⁶ On that day it shall be said to Jerusalem:
"Do not fear, O Zion;
  let not your hands grow weak.
¹⁷ The LORD your God is in your midst,
  a warrior who gives victory;
he will rejoice over you with gladness,
  he will renew you in his love;
he will exult over you with loud singing
¹⁸   as on a day of festival."
"I will remove disaster from you,
  so that you will not bear reproach for it.
¹⁹ Behold, at that time I will deal
  with all your oppressors.
And I will save the lame
  and gather the outcast,
and I will change their shame into praise
  and renown in all the earth.
²⁰ At that time I will bring you home,
  at the time when I gather you together;
yea, I will make you renowned and praised
  among all the peoples of the earth,
when I restore your fortunes
  before your eyes," says the LORD.

☙❧

God's Joy

Philippians 4:4-7 RSV

⁴ *Rejoice in the Lord always; again I will say, Rejoice.* ⁵ *Let all men know your forbearance. The Lord is at hand.* ⁶ *Have no anxiety about anything, but in everything by prayer and supplication with thanksgiving let your requests be made known to God.* ⁷ *And the peace of God, which passes all understanding, will keep your hearts and your minds in Christ Jesus.*

12.

God's Joy

Zephaniah 3:14-20; Philippians 4:4-7 RSV

Sometime in this Christmas season, we're going to sing a Christmas carol that begins,
> "While by the sheep we watched at night,
> glad tidings brought an angel bright."[52]

It's not one of the more popular or familiar songs, but you'll recognize it when you hear it. Each verse is just a sentence long—the emphasis is on the resounding chorus that follows:
> "How great our joy!
> Joy! Joy! Joy!"

Joy is a big part of the Christmas season. We work very hard to get ourselves in a good mood and to cheer each other up with lovely lights and warm wishes and being on our best behavior in case someone really *is* making a list of who's naughty and nice.

Everything about this time of year is geared toward raising the level of excitement and enthusiasm and "sense of the special," whether the "special" is spiritual or not. Everybody wants to get in

---

[52] From the hymn, "How Great Our Joy," traditional German carol, Theodore Baker (1851-1834), translator.

on the act of "accentuating the positive"[53] as Christmas approaches.

❧

We Christians, of course—being completely unfazed by the effects of the crass commercialism around us—confine our joy to the faith-based aspects of Advent and the coming of Christ at Christmas. Our joy is intended to be the holy kind—the kind we sing about in carols and look to in the lighting of candles symbolizing our joy—like the pink one that we began burning today.

And as Christmas Day grows closer—and the excitement builds—and we remember and retell the story of the salvation that arrived with the birth of the Baby in Bethlehem, we may—we should—find ourselves feeling what the words of that carol are saying:

"How great our joy!"

But have you ever considered: however great your joy at Christmas—however great our combined, corporate joy as Christians as we join our joy together—God's joy is—must be—infinitely greater? I would like for you to consider with me this morning: God's joy.

Oh, we think about a lot of the other traits and aspects of God. There is a song that goes,

"Think about His love.
Think about His goodness.
Think about His grace
that's brought us through."[54]

And we do think about our heavenly Father's great love and grace and goodness.

---

53 See "Ac-Cent-Tchu-Ate the Positive," Harold Arlen and Johnny Mercer, 1944.
54 From the song, "Think About His Love," Walt Harrah and John Newton, 1987.

But what about the joy of God? How great is God's joy over all that happened—that He caused to happen—at Christmas? We sing:

> "Joy to the world!
> The Lord is come…"[55]

Might it not be just as right to sing,

> "Joy to the Lord!"?

If this seems like a strange concept to consider regarding God, remember the remarkable message you just heard from Zephaniah:

> *"The Lord your God is in your midst…*
> *He will rejoice over you with gladness."*

And who is the "you" he's referring to?

God's people. The people who made God so mad with their misbehavior that He brought in the Babylonians to teach them a lesson and take them into exile.

If God can rejoice over them—sing and celebrate like the happiest person at a Christmas party because of them—if God can find joy in those people, why not in us, too? Is it possible that we could bring God joy, sinful as we are?

Apparently so, based on what the Bible says today.

But if so, how?

Maybe it works like this: though God wanted the world that He created—and every person and thing created in it—to be perfect (which is why He created it all—and us—perfect)—more than perfection, God wanted—and still wants—*us*—even in our terribly imperfect state.

God loves us! That part of the revelation comes across loud and clear. God wants relationship with us. That's what He created us for.

Yes, He hates sin—the sin in us—precisely because of what sin does to us and our world and our relationship with Him—the God Who created us to take joy in us. God could have wiped out

---

[55] "Joy to the World," Isaac Watts (from Psalm 98), 1719.

every sinner and every vestige of sin and started completely over and fixed the problem that cropped up in the Garden contrary to His instructions. He could have created a better bunch of people the second time around.

But God didn't want a second set of humans—He wanted the ones He created to begin with, whatever they did to mess themselves up. They—you—give God joy. Just existing, you give Your Creator immeasurable, indescribable, unending joy.

It's kind of like parents jumping through all kinds of holiday hoops to create a Christmas experience to captivate their kids. Why do they do it? And why do grandparents travel great distances to "be there" on Christmas morning? Why do they do it?

Because their children are their greatest joy—and seeing the joy on the little faces of those they love most is worth everything they can do to put it there.

And for the parents, it's not just about the actual events of Christmas morning. Unlike their children, they can anticipate what their children will actually experience—and how their children will react. And their parental anticipation of their children's joy brings them additional joy even before the time. Loving parents know things the children they love and adore do not know. Our loving heavenly Father knows things that we—the children He loves and adores—do not know.

We know that God sent His Son to be born a Baby to secure our salvation from this world and bring us safely home to heaven. It gave God great joy to send Jesus to rescue us. God knows even better than we what that truly means.

I suspect it gives God even greater joy to know what is still in store for us when He finally brings us home with Him to that place of perpetual Christmas we have never seen and cannot begin to imagine. God wants to be face-to-face with us to enjoy the look on our faces when we see His face for the first time—and we realize we will enjoy that face and that relationship for all eternity—with never ever a hint of the sin that strains our relationship with Him while we go about our business here and now.

You and I will rejoice forever "when we all get to heaven"[56]—even though the old hymn only talks about "what a day of rejoicing" the first day everybody gets there "will be." But our joy—on the first day and every day and forever—will be nothing compared to God's joy.

God has taken joy throughout the ages in the knowledge of what He was going to do to restore all His Creation to its primordial perfection in relation to Him. He took incomparable joy in sending His Son—joy His angels sensed and shared among themselves, and then with those who would be first and most directly affected: with Mary, and then Joseph, shepherds, and then the townsfolk, pious pray-ers and astute astrologers.[57]

The Father passed that joy on to the Son, in Whom He announced His pride and pleasure: *"This is my beloved Son, with whom I am well pleased"*[58]—or as we might put it today: "That's My Boy!"

And Jesus, we are told, *"for the joy that was set before him, endured the cross...."*[59] And He told His disciples the night *before* He went to the Cross, *"you have sorrow now, but I will see you again and your hearts will rejoice...."*[60] Like a woman in labor, when her baby is delivered, *"she no longer remembers the anguish,"* He said, *"for **joy** that a child is born into the world."*[61]

And so, with the birth of Jesus that first Christmas, God's joy was unbounded. And though witnessing the anguish of our Christ in His Crucifixion is painful even for the heavenly Father Who sent Him to give the greatest gift He could give us, God's joy was full again when He watched His Son come alive again in that second morning of holy birth we call Easter.

---

[56] From the hymn, "When We All Get to Heaven," E. E. Hewitt, 1898.
[57] Matthew 1—2; Luke 1—2.
[58] Matthew 3:17, RSV.
[59] Hebrews 12:2, RSV.
[60] John 16:22, RSV.
[61] John 16:21, RSV.

God's Joy

What joy God must take in the salvation of those who are lost and cannot save themselves! We rejoice in Him—and He rejoices in us. We rejoice together with our God.

⁂

There is a movie making the rounds of the theatres this holiday season that could be a perfect parable of this joy shared *"on earth as it is in heaven."* It is the story of what happened when a mine collapsed some years ago in Chile, in South America.[62] Thirty-three miners were trapped, deep within the earth, with no hope of getting themselves out of the deadly hole that could have easily become their grave. Thirty-three souls, barely able to keep themselves alive, waiting to be rescued, trusting in the powers above to save them, praying to God each day and all day during the months of their ordeal for the miracle that would raise them up.

Above them, their president came and ordered every resource in the nation to be used.

Help was brought from around the world. Just as the food ran out below, those who were lost were found. Those above them broke through to them—reached down to them—and from that day on, those trapped in the world below were given each day their daily bread—and more.

And one day, a person came down from above to be with them and help them, and with his helpers, ensure that they would finally be raised up.

Rejoicing already in anticipation, those who had been trapped each rose in their time to share a joyful reunion with their loved ones who had waited in hope for them. And they met the great leader who had arranged their rescue and who was just as joyful as they were to see them safely home. Joy flooded over them all—

---

[62] Movie *The 33*, 2015.

and over countless millions throughout the world, because the whole world had been watching—as had all of heaven, I am sure.

In the coming of Christ, the Leader of all sends His best Rescuer to those who cannot, through their own efforts, get out of their trap, and cannot survive for long within it. And their joy at their rescue cannot come close to matching the joy of the One Who ordered and organized and accomplished it.

The President of Chile made a promise at the beginning of the cave-in to get his countrymen out of their deadly peril if there was any way he and the world community could do so. The Lord of Creation made a promise at the beginning of sin to get every person (who will let Him) out of the clutches of sin, and safely secured in the heavenly home our Father has prepared for all of us. The President of Chile and God have both kept their promises and rejoice in being able to.

Like a warrior who has just won a great battle, the God Who is with us rejoices over us with gladness—He revels over us with songs of celebration.

And then Zephaniah changes the image of God's joy: like a mother marveling over her newborn baby, God quietly, silently, renews us in His love. A priceless picture of God's great paternal joy—in us.

One of the more familiar carols we sing each year is called, "O Come, All Ye Faithful." The words of the chorus extend an invitation:

"O come, let us adore Him."

That's a good idea, but according to Zephaniah, we might just as well sing,

"O come, let God adore us."

Joy! Joy! Joy! How great our joy!
And how greater still, His.

O Come, Let God Adore Us

Zephaniah 3:14-20 RSV

¹⁴ Sing aloud, O daughter of Zion;
   shout, O Israel!
Rejoice and exult with all your heart,
   O daughter of Jerusalem!
¹⁵ The LORD has taken away the judgments against you,
   he has cast out your enemies.
The King of Israel, the LORD, is in your midst;
   you shall fear evil no more.
¹⁶ On that day it shall be said to Jerusalem:
"Do not fear, O Zion;
   let not your hands grow weak.
¹⁷ The LORD your God is in your midst,
   a warrior who gives victory;
he will rejoice over you with gladness,
   he will renew you in his love;
he will exult over you with loud singing
¹⁸   as on a day of festival."
"I will remove disaster from you,
   so that you will not bear reproach for it.
¹⁹ Behold, at that time I will deal
   with all your oppressors.
And I will save the lame
   and gather the outcast,
and I will change their shame into praise
   and renown in all the earth.
²⁰ At that time I will bring you home,
   at the time when I gather you together;
yea, I will make you renowned and praised
   among all the peoples of the earth,
when I restore your fortunes
   before your eyes," says the LORD.

※

13.

O Come, Let God Adore Us

Zephaniah 3:14-20 RSV

We're encouraging you to read the Bible through in the coming year. If you do, you will eventually get to the Old Testament prophets. You'll read a lot of harsh words about gloom and doom in the prophetic books, which is understandable: if everything had been "peachy" in the history of God's people, there would have been no need for prophets to point out their sin or pronounce the punishment that was coming.

You'll read a lot about disaster and destruction—God's righteous judgment. But one day you'll come to the end of the Book of Zephaniah—to the passage you heard today. And you'll hear a prophet shouting for joy and telling you to do the same: "Celebrate! Throw a party!"

Is he out of his prophetic mind? No, he's just caught a vision of what comes *after* God's judgment upon the people God loves.

Some people don't want to bother with the Old Testament at all: "That God is so angry."

But when it comes to His people, the truth is that God's anger at them is an aspect of His love for them. You know what that's like. Haven't you ever been angry with a child or a spouse or a friend because that person, whom you love dearly, was doing something wrong? How about if that person violated the trust between you, perhaps repeatedly?

If you were angry, it was because you loved them. You were angry because, whatever else they were doing, they were hurting themselves and their relationship with you.

If God sounds angry in the Old Testament, it is a measure of His love. God's love for the people He has chosen to be His own is infinite, incomparable and unconditional. And there is no greater or more moving expression of God's love than these words:

> *"The Lord has taken away the judgments against you,*
> *He has turned away your enemies…*
> *He will rejoice over you with gladness…*
> *He will exult over you with loud singing…."*

Do you ever get to loving God so much that you just want to throw a party and celebrate—just sing out loud and celebrate with all your heart? Did you know that's how God feels about you? "Oh, how He loves you and me!"[63]

"I will remove disaster from you," says God. "I will deal with all your oppressors. I will save the sick and gather the outcasts among you. I will change your shame into fame. I will restore your fortunes before your eyes. I will bring you home."

Doesn't it make you want to sing? "Love divine, all loves excelling—joy of heaven to earth come down!"[64] Imagine the joy of heaven coming down to earth—to you. Imagine that the joy of heaven—God's joy—is because of you. Imagine God loving you so much that He just has to sing. Imagine God raising a cosmic cheer because you mean so much to Him.

And then imagine God loving you so much that nothing He could say would express His love for you. Your Bible says, *"He will renew you with his love."* But the Hebrew actually says, *"He will be silent in his love."*

---

[63] From the song, "Oh How He Loves You and Me," Kurt Kaiser, 1975.
[64] From the hymn, "Love Divine, All Loves Excelling," Charles Wesley, 1747.

The Third Sunday in Advent

Have you ever seen a fellow so much in love with his girl he just stared at her without saying a word? Have you ever seen a mother just stare at her new baby, adoring this one she created? The love is so strong that the one who feels it is silent.

Sometime this month, you will probably sing, "O Come, All Ye Faithful." The chorus goes,
> "O come, let us adore Him—
> Christ the Lord."

Like the shepherds who heard the choirs of angels singing "Joy!" and "Glory!" in celebration—like Mary adoring her Child—you and I, the faithful of this generation, come to Christmas—come to our Christ—singing songs of joyful praise because we love our holy God—our heavenly King.

But like Mary adoring the Christ Child Who has come to her—the God Who has come to us adores us—not because we are in any way adorable—but because our God is a God Who loves and adores. And He has chosen to make us—His people—the object of His great love.

In silent adoration—in full-throated celebration—God is loving us. O come, let Him adore us!

And in that same spirit of giddy, wonderful love: Sing! Shout! Rejoice! O come, let us adore Him.

The Fourth Sunday in Advent

The Christmas Problem

Matthew 1:18-25 RSV

[18] Now the birth of Jesus Christ took place in this way. When his mother Mary had been betrothed to Joseph, before they came together she was found to be with child of the Holy Spirit; [19] and her husband Joseph, being a just man and unwilling to put her to shame, resolved to divorce her quietly. [20] But as he considered this, behold, an angel of the Lord appeared to him in a dream, saying, "Joseph, son of David, do not fear to take Mary your wife, for that which is conceived in her is of the Holy Spirit; [21] she will bear a son, and you shall call his name Jesus, for he will save his people from their sins." [22] All this took place to fulfil what the Lord had spoken by the prophet:

> *[23] "Behold, a virgin shall conceive and bear a son,*
> *and his name shall be called Emman'u-el"*

(which means, God with us). [24] When Joseph woke from sleep, he did as the angel of the Lord commanded him; he took his wife, [25] but knew her not until she had borne a son; and he called his name Jesus.

14.

The Christmas Problem

Matthew 1:18-25 RSV

The coming of Jesus was a problem.

Understand: this was a time and place in which the rules of sexual behavior were strict and clear. They were also universally accepted and vigorously enforced. Primary among these rules was that young ladies getting married would not "be with child" before the wedding process was formally completed and the bride moved into her husband's household. *Any* time before *that* time was a *bad* time to turn up pregnant. It was not acceptable. In fact, it was downright scandalous.

This was no way to start a respectable family. Nor, would you think, was it a good way to start a new religious movement. It certainly doesn't look good. But maybe it can be explained. Just tell everybody: "It's not what it seems. I've not—we've not—violated the law against sexual intercourse before marriage. We don't really know how it happened, but we have been told by angels from God that a Child was placed in there by the Holy Spirit."

I wouldn't want to argue *that* case in the court of public opinion. Who would believe it? It's simply unacceptable. There's no way around it: the coming of Jesus was a big problem.

~~~

And for a lot of people, it still is.

Ours is a time and place in which all the rules of sexual behavior have been turned on their heads. The only rule left seems to be that everyone does what is right in his own eyes. But the unusual nature of the coming of Jesus is no more acceptable today that it was then.

The scandal today is in the story's "supernaturalism." Scientific research cannot confirm the objective accuracy of the story. Further, the story calls for the acceptance of the idea of the existence of a god—and not just any god, but a God with conscious and compassionate intentions—One with the power to reveal those intentions before the fact and to accomplish them in ways that radically affect human beings. To the modern mind, it's absolutely scandalous. This is not the way these things are supposed to be done. Religious things should be done decently and in order.

***

And so, as it turns out, Joseph's reaction is pretty normal. Mary's got something going on inside of her that Joseph would just as soon have nothing to do with. Poor Joseph! He wants to be a nice guy, but this really is too much—even for him. He doesn't want to be mean about it. He doesn't want to make a scene. But he does want to get away from it—far away—and fast. Joseph just wants to walk away from the problem, to pretend it isn't happening.

But it is happening, and normal human reactions—even polite ones—are the wrong way to go. Joseph's reaction isn't the right one, and God lets him know it.

How can you know what is right? How can you know when something that seems right, that everybody is telling you is right, that everything you've ever thought says is right, is really the wrong way to go? Joseph had a dream. Isaiah caught a vision. Elijah heard a still, small voice.

For each of them, God created problems—or what looked like problems—and then God spoke to them, and said, "Don't be afraid to accept the problem, to embrace it, to make it your own. Don't be afraid of what I'm doing in the lives of the people around you. Don't be afraid of what I'm doing in your life. And don't assume that what looks like a problem to you—is. I don't always do things the way people think I'm going to. And I certainly don't always do things the way people *want* Me to."

Things are not always what they seem when God is working out His will in human events. And God is not particularly concerned about how things look to the cynics of the world. In fact, it often seems that God rather delights in delivering His divine presents in unexpectedly humble wrapping. God delights in coloring outside the lines of the pictures we draw of Him. The truth is that Jesus comes to us in unexpected, even scandalous, ways, because that's the way God wants it to be.

Joseph didn't expect this—and neither did Mary. The problem for Joseph is not the temptation to do something evil, or to avoid an obvious good. As with many good people, the problem is the choice between two competing and worthy commitments. In Joseph's case, competing for his decision is his commitment to righteous obedience to God's commandments regarding moral purity, and his compassion for another person in trouble. Both are commendable driving forces, and under normal circumstances, your average woman would be very happy to find a man who possessed both traits. But these are not normal circumstances, and Mary is not your average woman.

And, of course, Joseph isn't the only one surprised: Mary hadn't factored this little surprise in when she was out there trying on wedding dresses. And it's bound to change her life forever, no matter how Joseph and everybody else respond. Joseph and Mary have both been taken off guard, but that's the way God wants it to be.

The Christmas Problem

They didn't expect "the problem" God had in mind for them, but they adjusted—and obeyed. Someone has said, "Life is what happens while you're making other plans." Both Joseph and Mary had lives, and they had plans for their lives. No doubt, they were planning to do the best they could with and for each other: go to work, raise a family, pay the bills. But God had other plans. He often does.

When God presents you with His plan, you can ignore it. Or try to. You can put on your blinders like an old mule and plow on ahead like nothing else matters but your plan.

I don't recommend that course of action.

Both Joseph and Mary, confronted by the problem of God's plan for their lives—or the problem that their lives were to be a part of God's plan—subordinated their plans to His. They adjusted their plans to His. They obeyed God. And their lives and the fate of the whole world changed forever as a result.

And their example is still useful for us today. Joseph, for instance, is told what God wants him to do and he does it. He is first told to take Mary as his wife. Then he is told to name Mary's baby, "Jesus."

Mary has throughout Christian history been seen as a symbol of the Church—or at least of the faithful Christian. And here we are told that she will bear—she will give birth to—she will deliver into the world—what is conceived in her—what God's Holy Spirit has caused to exist in her: the presence of God in human form. If we are to be like Joseph, we must accept God's direction to commit ourselves to those who bear the Holy One of God within them. Whether it be individual Christians or the church as a body, we are to be like Joseph and embrace them, love them, take them into our homes and our lives.

And God tells him to name the holy Child Mary bears, Jesus. Joseph had no part in creating Jesus, but he is authorized and empowered to identify Jesus to the world. You see, Joseph—legally—can make Jesus his own by acknowledging Jesus to the world, as his lawful son, simply by fulfilling the father's prerogative of giving Him a name. That's how God the Father acknowledges Him: by giving Jesus a Name (in this case, *the name that is above every name...in heaven and on earth and under the earth:* [65] *Yeshua*, Joshua, Savior). Joseph, as instructed, calls Him "Jesus"—"Savior"—and thereby makes Jesus his own.

Mary, too, adjusts and obeys God. Consider her example. Like Mary, the Christian (every Christian, by definition) is that one who *has* God—if not in physical form then in spiritual form—placed inside. And like Mary, the Christian is to experience that life of God within—to experience the growth of that divine Spirit within—until it is time to deliver It into the world. And as with Mary, this is not our doing, any of it. It is all the choice and power of God to work His will, in and through us.

You may find that people want to treat you like Joseph wanted to treat Mary when they find out what the Holy Spirit has conceived in you. You may find they want to put a little distance between themselves and you—without drawing a lot of attention to it, of course. But you can't let your worries about that get in the way of bearing Jesus to the world.

Joseph took Mary as his life's partner and named Jesus, Savior. Mary accepted the gift of God's Presence in her, allowed that Presence to grow and mature, and then delivered Jesus into the world to fulfill God's purpose. And look what came of "the problem."

"The birth of Jesus Christ took place...." Consider what incredible news this simple, basic statement of scripture is, all by itself. The "how" is interesting, but the *fact* that the birth took place is everything. It is the basis for everything else.

Because of this single, astounding fact, the revelation that followed became possible: *"He will save his people from their sins."* To save His people from their sins, JESUS MUST BE BORN.

---

[65] Philippians 2:9-10, NIV.

The Christmas Problem

But let's be clear on the purpose: Jesus will save His people from their sins. Yes, He provided instruction and inspiration. Yes, He had some great things to say about ethics and politics and stewardship. Yes, He healed the sick and fed the hungry, He cared for society's "losers," and valued little children. But His mission—the reason He was conceived in poor, young Mary's womb—was to save His people from their sins.

And that's why God has caused the Holy Spirit to be conceived in your wholly unprepared and inadequate body. *God was in Christ reconciling the world unto himself,*[66] and He is in you for the same reason today. The coming of Jesus was, as it turns out, not the problem it seemed to be, but instead a miraculous blessing.

And for a lot of people, it still is. You have an essential role to play in the ongoing miracle—the incredible blessing—that only *looks* like a problem. Do not be afraid to make a permanent commitment to God's plan for your life and to publicly identify Jesus as the Savior.

Anything else will really cause you problems.

---

[66] 2 Corinthians 5:19, KJV.

The Fourth Sunday in Advent

Isaiah 11:1-10 ESV

¹ There shall come forth a shoot from the stump of Jesse,
 and a branch from his roots shall bear fruit.
² And the Spirit of the Lord shall rest upon him,
 the Spirit of wisdom and understanding,
 the Spirit of counsel and might,
 the Spirit of knowledge and the fear of the Lord.
³ And his delight shall be in the fear of the Lord.
He shall not judge by what his eyes see,
 or decide disputes by what his ears hear,
⁴ but with righteousness he shall judge the poor,
 and decide with equity for the meek of the earth;
and he shall strike the earth with the rod of his mouth,
 and with the breath of his lips he shall kill the wicked.
⁵ Righteousness shall be the belt of his waist,
 and faithfulness the belt of his loins.
⁶ The wolf shall dwell with the lamb,
 and the leopard shall lie down with the young goat,
and the calf and the lion and the fattened calf together;
 and a little child shall lead them.
⁷ The cow and the bear shall graze;
 their young shall lie down together;
 and the lion shall eat straw like the ox.
⁸ The nursing child shall play over the hole of the cobra,
 and the weaned child shall put his hand on the adder's den.
⁹ They shall not hurt or destroy
 in all my holy mountain;
for the earth shall be full of the knowledge of the Lord
 as the waters cover the sea.
¹⁰ In that day the root of Jesse, who shall stand as a signal for the peoples— of him shall the nations inquire, and his resting place shall be glorious.

☙❧

Your Part in the Process

Matthew 1:18-25 RSV

[18] Now the birth of Jesus Christ took place in this way. When his mother Mary had been betrothed to Joseph, before they came together she was found to be with child of the Holy Spirit; [19] and her husband Joseph, being a just man and unwilling to put her to shame, resolved to divorce her quietly. [20] But as he considered this, behold, an angel of the Lord appeared to him in a dream, saying, "Joseph, son of David, do not fear to take Mary your wife, for that which is conceived in her is of the Holy Spirit; [21] she will bear a son, and you shall call his name Jesus, for he will save his people from their sins." [22] All this took place to fulfil what the Lord had spoken by the prophet:

*[23] "Behold, a virgin shall conceive and bear a son,
and his name shall be called Emman'u-el"*

(which means, God with us). [24] When Joseph woke from sleep, he did as the angel of the Lord commanded him; he took his wife, [25] but knew her not until she had borne a son; and he called his name Jesus.

15.

Your Part in the Process

Isaiah 11:1-10; Matthew 1:18-25 ESV

The angels are a busy bunch in the months leading up to—and the days after—the birth of Jesus, the Messiah. First, Zechariah, the elderly priest who will become the father of John the Baptist, gets a visit from an angel, right there at the altar in the Jerusalem Temple where he, Zechariah, is doing his priestly duty.[67] Then, another angel—the Archangel Gabriel himself, as it turns out—pays a visit to a virgin just going about her business in the Galilean village of Nazareth, just so she, Mary, will know that she is about to become the mother of the Baby Who will become the Savior of the world.[68]

An angel appears to shepherds outside Bethlehem the night that Jesus is born to tell them about it, and then an army of angels join the one, just to hammer the good news home.[69] Sometime later, it is an angel who tells the Wise Men that it won't be a good idea to go back and see King Herod after they have made the Messiah's acquaintance.[70]

---

[67] Luke 1:5-11.
[68] Luke 1:26-33.
[69] Luke 2:8-14.
[70] Matthew 2:12.

And right in the middle of all these miraculous messengers making their way earthward with words of wisdom for (almost) one and all, a carpenter with a conundrum falls asleep and receives a divine directive from an angel in his dreams. The man is named Joseph, after the famous Old Testament figure, and by the time he wakes up, this new Joseph will know what God would have him do about the business of the Baby his betrothed has been found to be pregnant with.

❦

Joseph, like his long-ago namesake, discovers in a dream that God is with him.[71] And He begins to perceive the part he is to play in the process of God's deliverance of His people.[72] For the old Joseph of Genesis, the deliverance would affect his whole family. For the new Joseph in Matthew, we're talking about nothing less than the salvation of the world.

Now, we know that Jesus is the Savior of the world. It is His birthday we celebrate at Christmas. He and He alone is worthy to become the Savior. He and He alone is the eternal and sinless Son of God Who will come to earth in the miracle of the Incarnation.

And yet, God enlists the service of Mary and Joseph—and shepherds and wise men and a host of angels—and a host of humans who are anything but angelic—to all play their different but essential parts in this prepared-from-the-foundations-of-the-world process to restore Creation—and humanity with it—to God's original plan. Every angel who talks to a person in the process of the birth of the Messiah is telling that person both what God is doing and what God wants him or her to do. Each person has a particular part—divinely assigned—in the process.

---

[71] Genesis 37:5-11.
[72] Genesis 50:20.

The Fourth Sunday in Advent

Look at Joseph, for example. He's a good guy, by all accounts—or by the biblical account, at least. He is committed to obeying God's law as he's been taught it. And though he is not without compassion for Mary and her "dilemma," Joseph wants no part in the process as it appears to be unfolding.

Don't get me wrong. Joseph wants to play a part in what God is doing. He believes in God and God's work. He just wants to pick the part he plays in God's plan himself—for himself.

Unfortunately—whether he knows it or not—the part Joseph wants to play with his life of faith is to remain safely on the sidelines. Trouble is: when you spend your spiritual life on the sidelines of faith, you can cheer others on as they play their part, but you can't play yours from there.

Now, let's be careful with this sports analogy, and make sure that I'm saying and you're hearing what the Bible is revealing. I'm not saying that not being able to do things—physically or financially, for example—is sitting on the sidelines, spiritually. I'm not saying that encouraging others is not one way to play your God-given part. It may very well be—encouragement is a genuine spiritual gift. After all, our God is not so cynical or cruel as to pick a part for you to play in His plan of salvation that you cannot play, and then hassle you spiritually because you're not playing it.

What I am saying is that everybody does have a God-given part to play in what God is doing in Jesus Christ. Mary does. Joseph does. You do.

And God will let you know what your part in the process is. Look at what God lets Joseph know.

❧

The first thing Joseph is told is that the part God has chosen for him to play in the life and work of Jesus may and must be accepted and accomplished courageously—without fear. "Do not fear to do what God wants you to do, Joseph," the angel says.

But "do not fear" what—or whom?

We usually think of Joseph being afraid of what other people will think of him if he weds a woman who is known to be pregnant before they finalize the marriage arrangements. And that's understandable; you know what it can be like in a small town. It is hard to embrace your part in God's process when peer pressure is pushing you to stay on the sidelines, away from the fray. But playing it safe is not playing your part.

More recently, there have been those who suggest Joseph is not so much afraid of what his neighbors will think, but of what life would be like for him with a woman who has become pregnant without the involvement of any man—since the Gospel of Matthew says Joseph knows that Mary's conception was a divine miracle. What would life be like as the husband of the woman who will give birth to the long-expected Messiah of God? What are you "in for" if the Child you raise as your own son is also the only-begotten Son of God? Joseph may feel he has more to fear from God than from anybody else.

Whatever Joseph is afraid of, the angel of God says, "Don't be." You don't have to be afraid of doing what God wants you to do, no matter how afraid you may feel.

శ—ళ

"Do not be afraid to take Mary as your wife."

Part of Joseph's part in the process of salvation is to take this other agent of God's will (Mary) into His life—to establish a relationship with her, within which—and because of which—the Messiah can be born and grow and fulfill His purpose.

Joseph's part in the process will bless Joseph—but it isn't about him. His part—and every part—is assigned—by God. And no matter how many blessings come out of it for the person playing it, the part is not assigned primarily for the benefit of the individual involved.

Your part in the process of God's salvation—like Joseph's—involves entering into redemptive relationships—first with Jesus—

and then with those who make up His family. It was a scary thing to commit ourselves to one another to become this church—this family of faith. It may have been scary, for you who have joined our fellowship since, to let us come into your life.

But we take the risk as we take one another as brothers and sisters in Christ so that Christ may live and grow in us. It is a part of our part in the process of salvation.

※

And the angel from God tells Joseph, *"call His name Jesus."*

The name "Jesus" means "Savior," and the role of the father in the biblical world is to tell the world who a child "is." To do this, a father gives a child a name. The Father Who has given this Child His name is His Heavenly Father, God Almighty, Who passes that "Name-above-all-names" on to the man God has chosen to be the father of Jesus on earth.

A part of your part in the process of God saving the world is to be one of the people who tells the world Who Jesus is—Who God has designed and defined Jesus to be—to call Jesus "Savior" and tell the world that He is the One God has sent to be *our* Jesus—*our* Savior.

But there's something more than passing on a name going on here. In the Bible, when a man names a child, he claims the child. A part of Joseph's part in the process of salvation is to claim Jesus as his Child—his Son—his Jesus—his Savior. A part of Joseph's part in the process is to show the world his personal commitment to this Child—and in so doing, to make Jesus the Son of David as well as the Son of God.

You see, Mary is related to priests and descendants of Levitical family lines, according to the Gospel of Luke. In the genealogy that begins the book of Matthew, it is Joseph who represents "the stump of Jesse"—the line of David—out of which will come the saving Shoot—the blessed Branch—foreseen by the Prophet Isaiah so many centuries before.

Of course, a God with the power to cause a virgin to conceive could have chosen any daughter of the house of David to carry and give birth to Jesus, just as easily as He chose Mary.

But it was God's inscrutable will to fulfill the prophecies in the way He did—through Joseph, a true male descendent of David, who will have to claim this Child as his Son—a Child that he had no part in conceiving—for the Child to become a son of David, as prophesied.

Every step along the way, ordinary people were given extraordinary parts to play in the process of God's salvation—ordinary people like you. In the approach to Christmas, as we cheer on the Savior Who came to earth in a miraculous combination of the impossible and the ordinary, remember that you, too, have a part to play in the process of salvation.

You are not to be afraid of the people who may misunderstand or oppose your obedience to God. You are not to be afraid of the work that will bring you into the very presence of God. You must not be afraid to live your life within—and committed to—the fellowship of faith—to embrace those the world rejects because of their vital connection to Christ.

You must boldly claim Jesus as your own—and proclaim Him as the Savior—and dedicate yourself to the role of raising Him up in your life where His presence and impact will grow ever stronger. That is your part in the process. That is God's Christmas wish for you.

16.

Christmas Almost Didn't Happen

Isaiah 11:1-10 (p. 101); Matthew 1:18-25 ESV (p.102)

Matthew writes in his Gospel, *"This is how the birth of Jesus the Messiah came about..."* But what follows is really the story of how the birth of Jesus the Messiah almost *didn't* come about. It is the story of how one man almost messed everything up, after what Matthew presents as God's meticulous work for hundreds of years setting everything up for the coming of the Christ.

Matthew makes it all look easy with his genealogy that lines everything up, from Abraham and the other patriarchs through David and the other kings to Joseph—with a few interesting women woven in here and there. But then, right when everything is finally ready to go—*after* everything is ready, really—Mary is already pregnant and the Baby is coming—so after everything is a "go," Joseph gets cold feet. And without Joseph, Christmas—the coming of the Christ—isn't going to happen—not the way God has intended—and prepared—for untold generations.

What's the problem?

It's hard to tell. Joseph is a good guy. Matthew says he's *"a righteous man,"* meaning he agrees with and plays by the rules—in this case, the rules God gave Moses for the Jewish people at Mount Sinai. Joseph is committed to doing the right thing; and marrying a woman who is already pregnant is *not* the right thing, according to the rules he goes by.

Joseph is a righteous man, but he is also kind and considerate, even when the rules don't require him to be. He shouldn't marry Mary, according to the rules; but he doesn't have to punish her—to make her situation harder than it's going to be anyway. So Joseph is working on the best way to split the difference—to get himself out of a fix without putting Mary into too much of one.

Of course, if Joseph doesn't play ball, Christmas as God intends it isn't going to happen. Maybe the whole "Christmas thing" just doesn't fit the way Joseph has been taught things are supposed to be done.

On the other hand, maybe it isn't the "outside the normal routine-ness" of it all—or the "what will other people think-ness" that has Joseph ready to pull the plug on the marital plans.

Maybe he's not trying to avoid marrying an already pregnant woman.

After all, Matthew says that Mary *"was found to be pregnant through the Holy Spirit."* Mary hasn't done anything wrong. But marrying a miracle mother might just bring too much religion into the life of a man who is willing to follow the rules and be nice if he doesn't have to get too directly involved in anything truly spiritual. Adopt the promised Messiah and raise Him as your own son and any chance of having a normal life is out the window. Marry Mary and it will be "God all the time all over the place." What kind of life is that?

And suppose you're not up to the task. Can you hear Joseph's mind working? "Maybe Mary *is* blessed among women. Maybe she *is* the handmaid of the Lord and the Child she is carrying *will* be the holy Son of God. But what about me?" Maybe Joseph does a little self-assessment and decides he's nobody special. "What does a carpenter know about raising a Christ? God is good, but suppose I goof it up?"

The Fourth Sunday in Advent

And so Joseph looks for a way out—a way that maybe won't make God any madder than Joseph going through with the marriage and then messing up the parenting of the Prince of Peace.

What's Joseph's problem? What's anybody's problem who has the chance to claim Jesus as his own—and take Jesus home—and make Jesus family—and spend his life with Jesus—and decides he doesn't want to?

Christmas Day is on the calendar. December 25th will come this year and lots of holiday stuff with it, but for a lot of modern Josephs (and "Josephines"), Christmas will not happen on December 25th—or any day—because they don't want the personal inconvenience or the social stigma or the spiritual intensity that getting involved with Jesus involves.

You know, parents around the world will move heaven and earth, figuratively anyway, to make sure that some kind of "Christmas" happens for their kids. They will get something special to give their babies even if they have to beg, borrow or steal it.

And yet the world is full of people who will refuse the greatest gift that heaven could give to earth—who will not have the Baby born in Bethlehem, no matter what. So many people celebrating a Christmas that didn't actually happen—for them—like it almost didn't happen for Joseph—or any of us.

So there's Joseph, pondering his Christmas problem, planning the wrong response to the wonder of God's grace, with all its ramifications for the rest of us—and God, Who has staked an awful lot on Joseph doing the *really* right thing rather than just the *apparently* right thing. There's God, stepping in to help Joseph let Christmas happen.

Matthew says God sends Joseph a message—in a dream—probably so it won't scare him to death like hearing directly from God when he is awake probably would. But God has Joseph hear His message in the dream from an angel, so that Joseph will get the message—and the motivation to do what God wants him to do.

And God packs a lot into that message:

The angel says: *"Joseph, son of David..."*

God's message is: "I know who you are, Joseph, who you really are. I know you better than you know yourself. I know what you're made of and what you have to give My Son—the One I am giving to you so that you can love and cherish Him all the days of your life."

The angel says: *"Do not be afraid to take Mary home as your wife..."*

God's message is: "Do not be afraid to do what I want you to do. Do not be afraid of what other people will think of you, or whether you are good enough to get the job done right, or how it will change your life or you."

The angel says: *"She will give birth to a son, and you are to give him the name Jesus..."*

And God's message to Joseph is: "Mary's got her part to do, and you've got your part to do, if Christmas is going to happen. Your part, Joseph, is to claim the Christ as your own and to identify Him to the world as yours and as the One Who saves."

❦

Now, here's a question for you: Do you suppose Mary and Joseph are the only people God has been sending Christmas messages to? Do you think God has been trying to get through to anybody else—sending angels—messengers—to anybody else who isn't yet on board with letting God make Christmas happen—really happen—in his or her life—in your life?

What is God saying? "Christmas is coming and I want it to happen to you. I know who you are and what you need. You don't have to be afraid of what accepting My Messiah will mean for you. Christmas will happen if you will let it, because I will send Jesus to you. I've been planning this and preparing this for a long, long time, and all you have to do is let Me give My Son to you."

"When Joseph woke up, he did what the angel of the Lord had commanded him." Joseph wakes up from his dream, but because of his dream—

because he has heard God's message in it—he "wakes up" in a deeper, more profound sense. He comes to his senses spiritually as well as physically. He does—not what the rules of his society require, or the desires of his heart direct—but what God has called him to do. Joseph makes Mary his wife and Mary gives birth to the Child and Joseph gives him the name "Jesus."

And Christmas happened—and continues to happen every time a "Joseph" wakes up to the Christmas message of God and acts accordingly, claiming the Christ and making the Messiah "family."

Matthew began his story—his Christmas story—this way: *"This is how the birth of Jesus the Messiah came about."* You could begin your Christmas story the same way, if Christmas has truly happened to you. The words that would follow would be different, for your story is different, unique to you, even if the result is the same—from God's perspective.

There are as many Christmas stories as there are Christians, and as many potential Christmas stories as people for whom Christmas has not happened, because Christmas can happen to anyone—and everyone. And anyone who will wake up to God and His message of His Messiah will have a Christmas story to tell.

Wake up to Jesus—make Him yours and take Him home—take Him to your heart—and Christmas will truly happen to you.

The Lord is With You

Luke 1:26--38 NRSV

[26] In the sixth month the angel Gabriel was sent by God to a town in Galilee called Nazareth, [27] to a virgin engaged to a man whose name was Joseph, of the house of David. The virgin's name was Mary. [28] And he came to her and said, "Greetings, favored one! The Lord is with you." [29] But she was much perplexed by his words and pondered what sort of greeting this might be. [30] The angel said to her, "Do not be afraid, Mary, for you have found favor with God. [31] And now, you will conceive in your womb and bear a son, and you will name him Jesus. [32] He will be great, and will be called the Son of the Most High, and the Lord God will give to him the throne of his ancestor David. [33] He will reign over the house of Jacob forever, and of his kingdom there will be no end." [34] Mary said to the angel, "How can this be, since I am a virgin?" [35] The angel said to her, "The Holy Spirit will come upon you, and the power of the Most High will overshadow you; therefore the child to be born will be holy; he will be called Son of God. [36] And now, your relative Elizabeth in her old age has also conceived a son; and this is the sixth month for her who was said to be barren. [37] For nothing will be impossible with God." [38] Then Mary said, "Here am I, the servant of the Lord; let it be with me according to your word." Then the angel departed from her.

17.

The Lord is With You

Luke 1:26-38 NRSV

Long before there were surveillance cameras and spy satellites—long before MapQuest and GPS—there was God, Who knew every inch of the world He had created and the location of every person to whom He had given life. And one day, this God sent an angel to the very spot in a little Middle Eastern village where one particular person happened to be. That person was a teenage girl named Mary.

God sent an angel to this girl because God had something He wanted her to know and something He wanted her to do. We know what God wanted her to know because the Bible tells us, and we know what God wanted her to do because she did it. And the rest is history.

Except it isn't, really—not all of it. What's happened since the angel gave God's message to Mary until now is history. But what is happening now and what will happen in the future because of what the angel told Mary and what Mary told the angel in reply is alive with power and possibility. It ain't over. It never will be.

Even the encounter between the angel and this Jewish peasant girl is not merely history. It is a pattern. It is the pattern for God's encounter with every person on the planet.

He sent His angel to the very spot where a particular group of shepherds were tending sheep outside a little Middle Eastern village called Bethlehem. God sent an angel to them because God had something He wanted them to know and something He wanted them to do.

God sent an angel to the very spot outside the city of Jerusalem where a particular tomb sat empty because God wanted a particular group of fishermen, tax collectors, and others to know something and do something.[73]

And guess what: God is still working with the pattern. God knows exactly where you are—geographically and spiritually. And He can send His messenger right to you. God had something He wanted Mary to know and something He wanted her to do. He has something He wants you to know and something He wants you to do.

The angel told Mary, *"The Lord is with you."* God wants you to know the same thing is true for you. He is with you. The encounter with Mary seems to have been private. Nobody else was watching. Nobody else knew what she saw and heard.

Nobody knows what you are seeing and hearing in your heart and mind. You've got a whole other life going on inside. You show the outside world whatever you show them, but it's just the tip of the iceberg of who you are and the life you are experiencing.

God is sending a message to that person inside you as He did to Mary: "I am with you." Whatever you think of your life or of the person you have become—or will yet become—God is telling you what He told Mary: "I am with you. I am not against you. I am not neutral about you. I favor you. I am positively disposed toward you. I want your best interest and your well-being."

That's what God wanted Mary to know and that is what God wants you to know. Put that on the scales of the ups and downs,

---

[73] Matthew 28:1-7.

the pros and cons, the joys and sorrows of your life. *"The Lord is with you."*

And what does God want you to do? God wants you to accept His gift of divine Life within you. God wanted Mary to accept the physical life of the Incarnate, Messianic Son of God in her womb. God wants you to accept the indwelling spiritual presence of God in your heart and mind and soul. God wants you to accept It and continually nurture It and deliver It mature and healthy into the world.

Mary got that one right: *"I am the servant of the Lord.* And I'm willing for Him to do with me what He wants to do." The angel tells her, *"The Lord is with you."* And she tells the angel, "I am with the Lord." The Lord sent her a message and we got the message because she gave birth to Jesus.

When you know what God wants you to know and are doing what God wants you to be doing, Jesus will grow in you. That's the pattern. That's the plan. That's the privilege you share with Mary—if you are willing to say, as she did, *"Let it be unto me, according to his word."*

Genesis 17:15-19 ESV

¹⁵ And God said to Abraham, "As for Sarai your wife, you shall not call her name Sarai, but Sarah shall be her name. ¹⁶ I will bless her, and moreover, I will give you a son by her. I will bless her, and she shall become nations; kings of peoples shall come from her." ¹⁷ Then Abraham fell on his face and laughed and said to himself, "Shall a child be born to a man who is a hundred years old? Shall Sarah, who is ninety years old, bear a child?"

¹⁸ And Abraham said to God, "Oh that Ishmael might live before you!" ¹⁹ God said, "No, but Sarah your wife shall bear you a son, and you shall call his name Isaac. I will establish my covenant with him as an everlasting covenant for his offspring after him.

ತ⊶ೃ

Luke 1:26-35 ESV

²⁶ In the sixth month the angel Gabriel was sent from God to a city of Galilee named Nazareth, ²⁷ to a virgin betrothed to a man whose name was Joseph, of the house of David. And the virgin's name was Mary. ²⁸ And he came to her and said, "Greetings, O favored one, the Lord is with you!" ²⁹ But she was greatly troubled at the saying, and tried to discern what sort of greeting this might be. ³⁰ And the angel said to her, "Do not be afraid, Mary, for you have found favor with God. ³¹ And behold, you will conceive in your womb and bear a son, and you shall call his name Jesus. ³² He will be great and will be called the Son of the Most High. And the Lord God will give to him the throne of his father David, ³³ and he will reign over the house of Jacob forever, and of his kingdom there will be no end."

³⁴ And Mary said to the angel, "How will this be, since I am a virgin?"

³⁵ And the angel answered her, "The Holy Spirit will come upon you, and the power of the Most High will overshadow you; therefore the child to be born will be called holy—the Son of God."

ತ⊶ೃ

18.

Impossible Child

Genesis 17:15-19; Luke 1:26-35 ESV

Most of the time, when people talk about an "impossible child," they mean a child who's hard to discipline—a behavioral problem. At least, that's how my teachers—at school and at church—used the term when they would talk with my parents about me when I was a child. But that's another story....

When the Bible talks about "impossible children"—and it talks about more than one—it doesn't mean "hard to handle."

In a time as far before the birth of Jesus as we are after it, God promised Abraham that his wife, Sarah, would give birth to a son. "Impossible!" Abraham snorted. "Ninety-year-old women can't have babies!" And when Sarah heard that God was predicting—promising—a pregnancy for her, she had the same reaction—though she tried to deny it when God called her out on it.

They were all agreed: Sarah having a child at her age was impossible. They all agreed—except God.

"You laugh when I tell you what I am going to do?" says God. "Fine! When this 'impossible' child is born, you call him 'Laughter'" (which is what the name "Isaac" means in Hebrew).

And then, the impossible happened.[74] And not only was a child born when it seemed humanly impossible, but the child became the otherwise impossible means to the fulfillment of promises so vast and momentous that they, too, would have seemed impossible—to Abraham, Sarah, Isaac and their descendants—had God not been the One Who made them—and made them come true…

…which is exactly what's happening when, all those many centuries later, a young Jewish girl, a virgin, betrothed but not yet married—a descendent of Abraham and Sarah through the child it was impossible for Sarah to bear (until she did)—a Jewish girl halfway in history between Sarah and us—experiences her own divine visitation, and receives her own supernatural promise that she will give birth to her own impossible Child—a Child even more impossible than the one Sarah had been promised and produced.

At least with Abraham and Sarah, impossibly old as they were to conceive a child together, there was a father's seed and a mother's egg. With Mary—who is certainly a more appropriate age for having children—there will be no man involved in the conception of the Child she will carry in her womb, which makes conception impossible, of course, even in our own high-tech era of artificial insemination.

God will merely "tell" Mary's body to conceive. He will speak this impossible Child into existence just as He spoke the first man—and woman—into existence—along with their world—in the Beginning.[75]

And God has a name for this impossible Child, just as He had a name for the child it was impossible for Sarah to bear. God's messenger to Mary tells her to call her Child: "Jesus"—"Savior."

Isaac's name was a reminder at first of the bitter laughter of two people who had been around so long that they could not believe God could or would do the impossible. And then "Isaac"

---

[74] Genesis 21:1-7.
[75] Genesis 1:26-27.

The Fourth Sunday in Advent

became the name of their joyful response to the child whose birth transformed their experience of the present and their perception of their past and their expectations for the future.

Their impossible child was proof that God would fulfill all the promises He had made for the future of their family.

They did not live to see God do the impossible things He promised to do through Isaac.[76] They did not live to see their son sire a nation. They did not live to see the many kings who descended from him. They did not live to see the Savior of the world Who claimed them as His ancestors, both by flesh and by faith.[77] But they were told by God that He would give them an impossible child, and finally, they believed God, and, because of their faith, all the other impossible things happened as well.

The promises God is making to Mary—of the Child she will carry, though it is impossible—and of the impossible things this impossible Child will do—are not just for the benefit of her family, as with Abraham and Sarah—not just for building a handful of people into a nation. God is promising the Savior of the world—to the world. Through her—Mary—all the world will be blessed.

Of course, at the very moment God's angel speaks to Mary of the impossible things that are about to happen—of the Savior of the world to be conceived within her—most of the world thinks there is already a much stronger claimant for that title: Caesar Augustus. And compared to the great and god-like Caesar, ruling the vast expanses of his empire from the incomparable capital of Rome, the idea that any Jew, peasant or aristocrat, could do anything that would affect the whole world, or even get its attention, would seem absolutely impossible.

And in that regard at least, nothing much has changed, despite all that has happened since Gabriel went to Galilee to let a young girl named Mary in on the impossible things God was about to do. You and I live in a time when more things are humanly possible

---

[76] Hebrews 11:11-13.
[77] Romans 4:13-21.

than at any time in the history of the world. And yet people are more convinced than ever that what is humanly *im*-possible is also impossible for God.

In fact, there are more people alive today than ever before who believe that the very existence of God is impossible. Mention God in public in any serious or reverential way and you will be met by the original Abrahamic response: derisive laughter. "How can anybody with half a brain believe there is a god in this day and age?! It's impossible and everybody knows it!"

And this is the world—these are the people—to whom God announces the coming of His impossible Child and the fulfillment of promises so impossibly wonderful that anyone who will believe Him will go from cynicism to celebration.

Look at God's pattern:

God tells people the impossible things He's going to do—the impossible Child He has brought into the world and will bring into their lives. He tells people—and invites them to believe in—the impossible, before He has accomplished it. And when they do, then God does the impossible. God brings the Isaacs and the Samuels[78] and the John the Baptists[79]—and finally, Jesus, of Whom there is only one—into the world to bless the world, and, ultimately, to save the world from itself.

Funny thing about these impossibilities God announces and then brings into being: If you believe God when He tells you He is going to do impossible things in your life—He does them.

If you doubt—if you laugh it off—blow God's good news off and don't believe—He doesn't do what He can do, and would do, if you believed as He calls you to—if you believed and then waited for the fulfillment of His promises.

God promised Sarah a child and all the promises that went with him. And, impossible as it was, Sarah bore Isaac. And her life was blessed forever after.

---

[78] 1 Samuel 1:19-20.
[79] Luke 1:57-66.

God promised Mary that she would give birth—as a virgin—to the Savior of the world.

And impossible as this was even to imagine, Mary told the angel, *"Let it be to me according to your word."* And, according to another Gospel, *"the Word became flesh and dwelt among us."*[80]

Impossible!

And yet, all who believe the promises of God revere Mary to this day—and, as it happens, have been given *"the power to become children of God."*[81]

It was impossible for God to establish and preserve His covenant people, from Abraham and Sarah throughout the centuries, so that the Messiah could come forth from these people, and this covenant, as God promised. It was impossible for Jesus to be born—as God promised. It was impossible for Jesus to be raised from the dead—as God promised. It is impossible for Jesus to come back to earth as the eternal King Who will grant eternal life to those who believe in Him, and decree eternal punishment to those who are convinced that these things are impossible and so live their lives committed only to the humanly possible, confident in the impossibility of the impossible.

But this is a God Who is not hampered or deterred by man's sense of what is impossible.

And we believe His promises of the impossible things to come because we have seen the impossible things God has brought to pass already, even to this day.

A virgin will conceive and bear a Son.

Biologically impossible.

The Child will be the Savior of the world.

Logically impossible.

This Jewish peasant will be great.

Socially impossible.

This human being will be the Son of the Most High God.

---

[80] John 1:14.
[81] John 1:12.

Theologically impossible.
God will give Him the throne of His ancestor, King David, and He will reign over the house of Jacob forever.
Politically impossible.
Of His kingdom, there will be no end.
Conceptually impossible.

And yet, that's what happened—and is happening—and will happen. But if you do not believe it when God tells you, it won't happen to you. It is impossible for this Child—this Christ Child—to be born in you if you do not believe God when He promises to put Jesus in your heart and life. It is impossible to live a new, transformed life in Christ if you do not believe that God can and will give it to you as He promised. If you wait until you can get your hands or mind around something that doesn't seem so impossible, you will miss out on all the impossible things God is promising you—and is prepared to provide you.

We did not read to the end of the angel's conversation with Mary this morning. Before he was done, Gabriel told her one of the greatest truths of the universe: *"...with God nothing will be impossible."*[82]

God does the impossible—all the time. There is no child that He cannot bring to life. There is no life that He cannot transform through the Child Whose coming at Christmas was supposed to be impossible, but wasn't. Take a lesson from Mary—and from Sarah: believe God, no matter how impossible it may seem, and see the impossible happen in your life—over and over again, forever and ever, Amen.

---

[82] Luke 1:37, RSV.

Micah 5:2-5a ESV

> ² *But you, O Bethlehem Ephrathah,*
>   *who are too little to be among the clans of Judah,*
> *from you shall come forth for me*
>   *one who is to be ruler in Israel,*
> *whose coming forth is from of old,*
>   *from ancient days.*
> ³ *Therefore he shall give them up until the time*
>   *when she who is in labor has given birth;*
> *then the rest of his brothers shall return*
>   *to the people of Israel.*
> ⁴ *And he shall stand and shepherd his flock*
> *in the strength of the Lord,*
>   *in the majesty of the name of the Lord his God.*
> *And they shall dwell secure,*
> *for now he shall be great*
>   *to the ends of the earth.*
> ⁵ *And he shall be their peace.*

19.

The One of Peace

Micah 5:2-5a ESV

As you know, this is the last Sunday before Christmas. Soon, men everywhere will begin shopping for presents for their loved ones. Fortunately for the family—and the economy—women have been gathering their gifts for months.

Gift giving is central to our celebration of Christmas. Most of whatever support the secular world is still willing to give to Christmas these days is focused on promoting the purchasing of presents—more presents and more expensive presents. It's very big business.

It may sound like I'm getting ready to condemn this business of Christmas gift giving. I'm not—especially since I haven't gotten all of mine yet.

But I would like to clear away a bit of the commercial clutter so that we can see Christmas giving in a better light.

For instance, the original justification for giving Christmas gifts comes from the Bible—from the wise men in the gospel of Matthew who brought three gifts to give to the newborn King of the Jews they were seeking.[83]

---

[83] Matthew 2:1-12.

If you recall, these foreigners followed a star, first to Jerusalem where, unlike most of us men, they stopped and asked for directions. Then they headed down to the village of Bethlehem, about five miles south of the city, where they found the baby Jesus and laid their treasures before Him.

The Bible says they went home a different way, but I would like for us to double back to Jerusalem and revisit the visit they had with Herod and his biblical brain trust.

The wise men asked Herod where the new king of the Jews was. Herod, who was the current king of the Jews, did not know the answer because he did not know Jewish scriptures. But he did know that he now had some new competition and he wanted to get rid of it—quickly.

He called in the Temple crowd—the top dogs in the Jewish religious establishment—and gave them a one-question pop quiz: "Where is the Christ—the Messiah—to be born?"

They didn't have to do any research; they knew the answer already. Every real Jew knew the answer: Bethlehem! The little town of Bethlehem. *"From you, O Bethlehem of Ephrathah, shall come a ruler who will govern my people Israel."*

They knew the answer to Herod's question because they knew the scripture. But because they knew the scripture, they knew more than that. They knew what God promised centuries before.

They quoted from memory a passage from the prophet Micah—today's text, in fact. They knew these words of Micah by heart because they and all Jews had set their hearts on these words. They had held on to Micah's prophecy for centuries because it contains—for lack of a better term—"God's Christmas gift list."

And that's the point of this long and circuitous introduction: not the gifts we give for Christmas—not even the gifts the wise men gave Jesus that first Christmas—but the gifts that God gives us in Christmas—the gifts He gives us in giving us Christ.

The Fourth Sunday in Advent

Micah and his contemporary, Isaiah, live in a dark time. Their people have turned away from God. Their culture is immoral and their leaders are corrupt and ineffective. Enemies threaten them from many directions. Their world is falling apart, and they sense the coming of God's judgment. God is going to settle accounts with a rebellious and disobedient people.

Micah and Isaiah know their people have it coming and so they prophesy, so that when God's judgment does come, the people will know what hit them and why.

But the surprise is what comes after. God speaks through Micah and says, "From the little village where David was born, from Bethlehem in Judah, another like David will come."

"He will come first to Me," says God, "to show that He is totally submitted to Me and My purpose, and then I will make Him ruler over Israel."

What does God mean by "Israel"? Not another petty king of Judah. Not even a king over David and Solomon's old united realm. But "Israel." The real Israel. God's chosen people. All of them who know this God as their God—all of us who know this God as our God—to the ends of the earth.

When every child of God deserves a crushing load of coal in the stocking of his soul because of sin, God promises His children instead a Leader Who will protect them and provide for them and give them peace.

And this is no wait-till-the-last-minute, grab-whatever's-left-on-the-shelf-and-go kind of gift. What God has on His gift list was planned ages before Micah came along to hear about it and proclaim it. God was preparing this present "from of old—from ancient days—from the very beginning."

God is giving us Someone to lead us and take care of us Who is as strong as God Himself. Micah says, "The One that God will give you to rule over you shall stand in the strength of the Lord." Nothing can trip Him up or knock Him down.

Paul put it this way, *"...neither death, nor life, nor angels, nor principalities, nor things present, nor things to come, nor powers, nor height, nor depth, nor anything else in all creation, will be able to separate us from the love of God in Christ Jesus our Lord."*[84]

Whatever you have to face in your life, the One that God has given you is stronger. Whatever you are afraid of, the One that God has given you can overcome it. Is there something you just can't stand up to? The One that God has given you can stand up to it for you—because He stands in the strength of the Lord.

And while you're opening that present, I want you to see another one. The One that God has given you stands in the strength of the Lord to protect you—and—He feeds His flock in the strength of the Lord. God's Christmas gift list includes divine provision.

Your God shall supply all your needs. There are no deficits in God's benevolence budget. There is no debt He cannot pay—no debt that He has not paid. The Christ God has given you has paid all debts and still has infinite assets to provide for you. He will feed you as a shepherd feeds the sheep he knows and loves.

"Nice talk, Preacher. But what about all the bills piling up? What about all the people out of work right now?"

Yes, this is a time of struggle and uncertainty from the world's perspective. But God's Christmas gift is the promise of a divine provision that will not make sense to the world.

Jesus says, *"...do not be anxious about your life, what you shall eat or what you shall drink, nor about your body, what you shall put on.... ...your heavenly Father knows that you need them all. But seek first his kingdom and his righteousness, and all these things shall be yours as well."*[85]

Micah says, the One that God is giving us *"shall stand and feed his flock in the strength...and majesty...of the Lord..."* and as a result, *"they shall dwell secure."*

---

[84] Romans 8:38-39, RSV.
[85] Matthew 6:25, 33, RSV.

Security is one of the Christmas gifts God is giving you. We honor and appreciate those who provide for our security on foreign battlefields and in our local neighborhoods. They set aside their own security to ensure ours.

And yet, there is a limit to what their sacrifices can attain. You may still become a victim. You may still suffer injury or loss. And the security these wonderful men and women provide is, ultimately, only physical.

The One that God gives you secures your soul for all eternity, and in doing so, secures your spirit here and now by causing you to know that you are where you are supposed to be in relation to God. Paul says, *"the peace of God...will keep your hearts and minds in Christ Jesus."*[86] That's security.

God is giving His people a Ruler with an eternal pedigree. He is giving us a Leader Who can stand up to anything and provide for every need. God is giving us a divine Shepherd Who makes us dwell secure.

And God is giving us peace.

"He shall be the One of Peace," says Micah. Isaiah calls this One that God is giving us *"the Prince of Peace."*[87] What kind of peace are we talking about? Paul says, *"...we have peace with God through our Lord Jesus Christ."*[88] God is giving us One Who reconciles us to God—makes us right with God—makes peace between God and us.

And He makes peace between us and other people. *"Let the peace of Christ rule in your hearts,"* says Paul, *"since as members of one body you were called to peace."*[89] That we can get along with anybody in this broken world is a sign of His peace. That we are able to love one another despite our differences is simply the power of the Prince of Peace at work among us.

---

[86] Philippians 4:7.
[87] Isaiah 9:7.
[88] Romans 5:1, RSV.
[89] Colossians 3:15, NIV.

That we can be at peace with ourselves is another sign of this Christmas gift of God. Jesus tells His disciples, *"Peace I leave with you; my peace I give you. ...I have told you these things, so that in me you may have peace."*[90]

Amid all the feverish activity of giving and getting gifts this Christmas, listen to an age-old prophecy of God's Christmas giving to you: protection and provision, security and peace—yours in the One that God has given you at Christmas—for Christmas—as Christmas. When you're finished at the mall—when you've wrapped and then unwrapped all your gifts—"come to Bethlehem and see" (God's Christmas gift to you): "Christ the Lord, the newborn King."[91]

"Gloria in excelsis Deo!"[92]

---

[90] John 14:27; 16:33, NIV.
[91] From the carol, "Angels We Have Heard on High," verse 3, James Chadwick, 1862.
[92] The phrase is Latin for "Glory to God in the highest."

Luke 1:46-55 RSV

⁴⁶ And Mary said,
> "My soul magnifies the Lord,
> > ⁴⁷ and my spirit rejoices in God my Savior,
> > ⁴⁸ for he has regarded the low estate of his handmaiden.
> For behold, henceforth all generations
> > will call me blessed;
> > ⁴⁹ for he who is mighty has done great things for me,
> > and holy is his name.
> ⁵⁰ And his mercy is on those who fear him
> > from generation to generation.
> ⁵¹ He has shown strength with his arm,
> he has scattered the proud
> > in the imagination of their hearts,
> ⁵² he has put down the mighty from their thrones,
> > and exalted those of low degree;
> ⁵³ he has filled the hungry with good things,
> > and the rich he has sent empty away.
> ⁵⁴ He has helped his servant Israel,
> > in remembrance of his mercy,
> ⁵⁵ as he spoke to our fathers,
> > to Abraham and to his posterity for ever."

20.

Magnify and Rejoice

Luke 1:46b-55 RSV

What if you were the only person in the world who knew what God was up to? Suppose you were the only person who knew how and when God was going to do the biggest, most wonderful and significant thing He had ever done since the Creation of the world itself?

And you really knew! You didn't just have a hunch; you weren't guessing or putting a few clues together—God had come right out and told you. Imagine that one day, God showed up—or sent an angel—and you heard: "Here's what's going to happen—and you're going to be right at the heart of it."

If you were that person, you would probably want to tell somebody—after recovering from the shock. And, after recovering from the shock, that's what that person did.

In a modest house in an unnamed village in a remote region of the Roman Empire, two pregnant women are talking about—what else? The babies they are carrying. One woman is old—too old, you would think, to have a baby, except that the evidence is right there in front of her, so to speak.

The other woman is young—almost too young, or if not that, somehow too innocent, seemingly, to have become pregnant. And

Magnify and Rejoice

though she is not showing the signs as yet, she is sure of her condition. She has it on the best authority. The younger of the two women is that one unique person in all the world who knows exactly what God is doing.

The young woman—girl, really—is named Mary. And she is unique in all the world—and all of history—for another reason. She *is* as innocent as she appears. She is a virgin, and yet, she carries a child. And she knows that through the Child she carries, God is about to do the most wonderful thing that He has ever done for all the babies who ever were—or will be—born on the earth He created. She knows this because God told her so.

And so she goes to tell somebody who will understand. Mary tells someone close—a kindred spirit—someone who will celebrate with her, because knowing that God is doing the most wonderful thing in the world is reason for rejoicing. Knowing what she knows—experiencing what she is experiencing already—is enough, even before the Baby arrives, to make you sing for joy.

And Mary does. What you heard from the Gospel reading a few minutes ago was the first Christmas carol ever sung. It is called the *Magnificat*, because, in the Latin translation, that is the first word of what Mary sang. As the glorious good news from the angel of God began to sink in, even a girl as young and innocent as Mary began to appreciate what it was going to mean—for her and for her people, the poor, hungry, oppressed and yet faithful followers of the God of their fathers—and, ultimately, what it would mean for all the world. Wonder and amazement, overwhelming joy over what was now certainly going to happen—even if it had not yet.

What can you do but sing? And Mary's heart draws from all the hopes and dreams of her heritage of faith, and words of praise well up within her and pour forth:

"My soul magnifies the Lord
And my spirit rejoices in God my Savior!"

You go, girl! Sing it out!

The Fourth Sunday in Advent

Centuries before the familiar phrases of "Silent Night" and "Away in a Manger" ever graced the lips or warmed the hearts of millions of believers in every corner of the world, one young and unique handmaiden of the Lord raised her voice to "magnify and rejoice."

"My soul magnifies the Lord,"

Mary sang.

The angel of God told her,

"You are highly favored.
The Lord is with you.
You will…give birth to a Son…
[Who] will be great
and will reign over the house of Jacob—
you and your people—forever."

And this remarkable message permeated her whole consciousness and made her realize that whatever she thought of God—it didn't begin to do God justice.

The Lord—the Mysterious and Powerful Presence Who had made Himself known through His gracious miracles to His covenant people from Abraham to Moses to David and down through the centuries to Mary herself—was so much more than she could ever imagine.

And now, confronted with this reality, she had to "magnify" her understanding of Him.

She had to let the Lord God "grow" in her soul, just as Jesus, the Son of God Who was conceived in her, would grow in her womb.

The angel God sent to Mary told her God's Holy Spirit would come to her and overshadow her and cause her to carry a Child—she would carry a Child and yet remain a virgin.

And having experienced the presence and power and impact of the Holy Spirit on her body, she discovered, as well, the relationship that now filled her spirit with that Holy Spirit.

Magnify and Rejoice

God had made Mary His instrument to bring His salvation to her and to the rest of the lost and hopeless world through the Son that she would bear. She and they—everyone who believes and accepts the Holy Child God had placed within her—would be saved.

"God has sent His Savior and He's growing in me!"

"Happy" doesn't begin to tell it. You ought to be absolutely thrilled! Mary is:

"My spirit rejoices in God my Savior!"

...magnifying Who God is, and rejoicing over what God has done.

Of course, Mary's not the only one singing about the birth of Jesus. The first two chapters of Luke almost sound like a church musical with all the lyrics being lifted to heaven. Simeon holds the baby Jesus in the Temple and breaks into a song celebrating the goodness of God to let the old man live long enough to see the promised Savior.[93] The angels offer up their "glorias" in the skies over Bethlehem on the night Jesus is born.[94] John the Baptist's father, Zechariah, will celebrate his son's birth and future relationship with Jesus—after God gives him his voice back.[95]

But Mary's song is the first, and her joy and celebration come long before her Son is born. And that's the nature of Christmas joy: it comes to us even in anticipation. Just the knowledge that Jesus is coming—the very promise of salvation—sustains our hope and supplies our joy.

Mary sang about all the generations that would call her blest. And, generation after generation, we have. Mary celebrated the mercy of God that extends to those who fear Him from generation to generation—which includes our generation.

---

[93] Luke 2:29-32.
[94] Luke 2:14.
[95] Luke 1:66-79.

And in our generation, we join Mary and all those who have gone before us in faith, magnifying the Lord and rejoicing in our Savior. We cannot celebrate Christmas aright unless our souls are filled with the presence of the Lord, ever growing and expanding in our understanding and experience. We cannot respond properly to God's gift of His Son to save us until our spirits are so aware of the Holy Spirit's overshadowing presence that we sense with overwhelming joy the Savior Himself within us.

Mary was the first who sang the praises of God for the gift of His Son, Jesus. She was the first to feel the presence of Jesus dwelling within her. She was the first to receive God's message that His Son was being born.

Mary was the first—and for a time, the only—person in the world to be told how and when God was going to do the biggest, most wonderful and significant thing He had ever done since the Creation of the world itself.

Mary was the first to know, but she was not the last. Mary was the only virgin to give birth to the Son of God, but she is no longer the only person who has experienced the overshadowing power of the Holy Spirit and the indwelling presence of the Savior. Every believer has been overshadowed by the Holy Spirit. Every one of us carries the Christ Child inside. Every Christian *is* a Christian because we ourselves have heard and believed what Mary heard from the angel and believed. Every one of us has the same song of joy and wonder to sing—in response to the awesome saving act of God in Jesus—that burst forth from the fullness of Mary's heart.

When you know what we know—when you have what we have inside us—how can you not sing?

> *"My soul magnifies the Lord*
> *and my spirit rejoices in God my Savior"*
> for He has been mindful
> of my humble, sinful, hopeless condition.
> *"My soul magnifies the Lord*
> *and my spirit rejoices in God my Savior"*

> for [He] has done great things for me.
> He has lifted up the humble.
> He has filled the hungry with good things.
> He has helped His servant Israel...
> the people who believe His promises.

God has given me something to sing about, just like He did with Mary and all the rest. What God told Mary would happen either has or will. We know what God is doing and we know that He has put us right at the heart of it.

What is God doing? He's giving us Jesus so He can live and grow within us. God is giving us His Christmas gift.

"But it isn't Christmas yet."

Maybe not, but it will be soon and my heart still wants to sing—my soul wants to magnify—my spirit wants to rejoice—because God's Holy Spirit has put enough Jesus in me for me to believe His promise that the rest is on the way.

Christmas Eve

The Traditional Christmas Reading from the Gospel of Luke

Luke 2:1-20 KJV

¹ And it came to pass in those days, that there went out a decree from Caesar Augustus that all the world should be taxed.

² (And this taxing was first made when Cyrenius was governor of Syria.)

³ And all went to be taxed, every one into his own city.

⁴ And Joseph also went up from Galilee, out of the city of Nazareth, into Judaea, unto the city of David, which is called Bethlehem; (because he was of the house and lineage of David:)

⁵ To be taxed with Mary his espoused wife, being great with child.

⁶ And so it was, that, while they were there, the days were accomplished that she should be delivered.

⁷ And she brought forth her firstborn son, and wrapped him in swaddling clothes, and laid him in a manger; because there was no room for them in the inn.

⁸ And there were in the same country shepherds abiding in the field, keeping watch over their flock by night.

⁹ And, lo, the angel of the Lord came upon them, and the glory of the Lord shone round about them: and they were sore afraid.

¹⁰ And the angel said unto them, Fear not: for, behold, I bring you good tidings of great joy, which shall be to all people.

¹¹ For unto you is born this day in the city of David a Saviour, which is Christ the Lord.

¹² And this shall be a sign unto you; Ye shall find the babe wrapped in swaddling clothes, lying in a manger.

¹³ And suddenly there was with the angel a multitude of the heavenly host praising God, and saying,

¹⁴ Glory to God in the highest, and on earth peace, good will toward men.

¹⁵ And it came to pass, as the angels were gone away from them into heaven, the shepherds said one to another, Let us now go even unto Bethlehem, and see this thing which is come to pass, which the Lord hath made known unto us.

¹⁶ And they came with haste, and found Mary, and Joseph, and the babe lying in a manger.

For Christmas Eve and Christmas Day

[17] And when they had seen it, they made known abroad the saying which was told them concerning this child.
[18] And all they that heard it wondered at those things which were told them by the shepherds.
[19] But Mary kept all these things, and pondered them in her heart.
[20] And the shepherds returned, glorifying and praising God for all the things that they had heard and seen, as it was told unto them.

21.

Where Are You Going for Christmas?

Luke 2:1-20 KJV (p. 142)

If you were to ask people, "Where are you going for Christmas?" you might get any number of answers. If you were to ask, "Where are you going for Christmas in the Bible?" the most likely answer would be Luke, Chapter 2. Tonight, the likely answer is the right answer, for I am, in fact, going to Luke, Chapter 2. And you are invited to join me there.

ಌ

Christmas is a busy time—for most of us. Everybody is on the go. And no one is on the go more, during the Christmas season, than military people. Service men and women tend to have a long way to go—and not much time to get there. The common question this time of year is, "Where are you going for Christmas?" We expect that everybody is going somewhere for Christmas.

Mary and Joseph are going to Bethlehem—but they don't really want to. The roads are bad—and Mary is pregnant—and Joseph doesn't have the money to pay for the trip. But they're going to Bethlehem anyway—because they have to. The "shakers and movers" of the world don't even know they exist, but from half a world away, powerful people have set events in motion that will force Mary and Joseph to go to Bethlehem—for Christmas.

The Bethlehem they're going to isn't exactly filled with the holiday spirit. Lines are long and nerves are frayed. Traffic is terrible. It's pure Bedlam—a teeming tangle of strangers trying to make do with too little space and too few resources. And Mary and Joseph are among those "making do." They make the best of a bad situation, going to a stable with a manger—in Bethlehem—for Christmas.

And here's a funny thing: this strange and inconvenient—this costly (they're not on per diem orders, you know) and even dangerous—turn of events—instigated by the Roman Emperor himself, appears to serve the purposes of their God to a tee, as though God had planned it, rather than Caesar. As Joseph and Mary live out their lives in the daily push and shove of the indifferent world around them, they are, at the same time and through the self-same events, being positioned perfectly to serve the greater and deeper divine will of God.

Imagine: a God Who takes the workings of the material world and bends them to His grand design. Imagine: the burdens, difficulties, and disappointments of ordinary people like Mary and Joseph (and maybe you and me?) being the stuff God uses to bring about His salvation. You think you're just going about your business—living your life—and all the time, God is at work in it. It's kind of like old Jacob waking up one day and realizing, *"...the Lord is in this place and I didn't know it!"*[96]

Mary and Joseph go to Bethlehem under truly awful conditions—and a truly glorious thing happens. Their helplessness in the world serves to enable God to change that world. Going to Bethlehem doesn't seem like a Christmas trip to Mary and Joseph—not until they get there. It's only after they get to Bethlehem that Mary and Joseph discover that they have been

---

[96] Genesis 28:16, RSV.

going to Bethlehem—not for the census—but for Christmas. Funny how God works.

And Mary and Joseph aren't the only ones going to Bethlehem for Christmas. Shepherds are going, too. God sent an angel to announce the good news of the gospel to a bunch of shepherds somewhere outside the city limits, and they decide to go to Bethlehem and have a look.

But why shepherds? Mary and Joseph, you can understand: they're nice people—and religious. Shepherds, on the other hand, are dirty. And they smell bad. They trespass on other people's property. Why doesn't God "drop" the good news on the good people of Bethlehem—people with a little more credibility and standing in the community—people with a little more sophistication—and better table manners? Why doesn't God send angels to…well, to people like us?

Maybe God's good news isn't just for good people. Maybe God doesn't need or want the good news to depend on anyone's earthly credibility. Maybe people with a little more sophistication wouldn't believe their own eyes and ears if they saw an honest-to-goodness angel, regardless of what the angel said. I mean, newborn babies are pretty common, but angels in the sky rank right up there with space aliens and UFOs.

Maybe God picked shepherds because you just might need to be a little gullible to believe that the good news about Jesus in true. You can't very well believe the good news is true if you're not willing to believe that the good news *could* be true. And today, anyone who doesn't reject the gospel of Jesus—on principle—is considered hopelessly gullible. Believe that God could be at work in our world and our lives and you could be dangerous to the wellbeing of your community—according to those who are too sophisticated to be taken in by such superstitious nonsense.

(I sometimes wonder whether, on the whole, hell might turn out to be a more sophisticated place than heaven, given how many of the smart people in our world reject Jesus, while so many simple, humble folk joyfully embrace Him. Just a thought...)

The shepherds saw an angel—and heard something wonderful. And a multitude of angels (or "heavenly host," if there's a difference) came along just to make some noise of the "glorifying and praising" variety.

On the other hand, nobody else in or around Bethlehem seems to have heard or seen anything out of the ordinary. Of course, it's not that unusual for somebody to see the evidence of God's activity while the rest of the world sees nothing. It happens to Christians all the time.

Anyway, Mary and Joseph have to go to Bethlehem—but the shepherds don't. You could even make a pretty good case that they shouldn't. They have flocks to watch out in the fields. They have responsibilities. The shepherds have plenty to do without making a trip into Bethlehem. And Bethlehem right now is a madhouse. Isn't it enough just to know the Christmas story without you having to do anything about it?

Apparently not.

The angel said there was something to see. The angel said there was a sign. And the thing about signs (the ones from God, anyway) is that you don't get to see the sign until you respond properly to the revelation the sign is provided to confirm.

"Show me the sign."

"You'll see it when you see it."

"Well, that's a big help."

"It's the way God does business."

When you do what God tells you to do, you find that you really are doing what God tells you to do, but you only find out if you do it, and not until you do.

But it wasn't much of a sign anyway: "You will find a baby that has been born in a barn." Big deal! What's so "God-in-heaven" impressive about that? Mall decorations are more impressive. Houses in my neighborhood—and yours too, probably—look more like "Christmas" than that stable with the Christ-Child in it does.

You may be looking for impressive stuff from God, but a lot of God's signs are just like this one: normal, everyday stuff to everybody else, but "God-in-person" to those who know what to look for—and are actually willing to get up and go look.

The sign itself is no big deal because God is not so concerned about looking impressive as He is about being effective. And God is very, very effective in providing a Savior for a whole world lost in sin and condemned to hell. Providing a Savior would actually make what God is doing more impressive, say, than the mall, even though it doesn't look like it on the surface.

And listen to what the angel had to say:

"I bring you good news....
to you is born...a Savior...
...this will be a sign for you...
you will find a Baby..."

Sounds like they've won the biggest lottery jackpot ever—without even buying a ticket—which is exactly what they've done. But they don't have to respond to the good news. Given the news, though, it's hard to imagine anybody not wanting to.

As it turns out, nothing the shepherds have to do is as important as going and seeing that one...little...Baby in a manger.

If you were to measure, the field they came from isn't really that far from the manger. But when the shepherds arrive there in Bethlehem, they find themselves in a whole different world. And though the fields they will go back to are the same old fields, the lives they will go back to will be forever new.

The shepherds hear and go and see, and when they see, they tell what they have heard and seen, which causes others to hear, and to decide whether they will go to see what they've heard about, just like the shepherds did. If these people do go and see, they will have something to tell still other people, who, when they hear, may decide to "check it out" for themselves, and on it goes. Hear. Go. See. Tell. Hear. Go. See. Tell.

Who do the shepherds tell? Oh, whoever is there—whoever they run into—whoever will listen. The shepherds even tell Mary and Joseph what they have heard out in the fields, since the angel didn't come to the manger. Funny how revelation works. But, of course, Mary and Joseph have seen and heard even more than the shepherds have.

Mary and Joseph are going to Bethlehem for Christmas because of an imperial order. The shepherds are going to Bethlehem for Christmas because of an angelic proclamation. But there is Another Who is going to Bethlehem for Christmas, and He goes because a sinful humanity desperately needs Him to.

The sin of mankind requires atonement. Our alienation from God requires a reconciliation only He can accomplish. And so God is going to Bethlehem for Christmas, or better yet, to "become" Christmas, to atone for and reconcile sinners like you and me.

The time came for Mary to give birth, and she did. That's about all Luke has to say about the actual birth of Jesus. It happened. It was not a good time for it, by all human reckoning, but the time came, and Jesus came, which means God came. God Himself came—to Bethlehem—for Christmas. God came to us, and not just to the good among us—or the powerful. God came as a Baby born to nobody special (by worldly standards) and spends His first hours of human life in a borrowed manger in a rented stable in a village on the outskirts of the civilized world that won't even be His hometown. And what does it mean? It means that now God is with us and God is for us because God has become one of us.

The birth of Jesus, the coming of God in human form, doesn't look much like the incredible miracle it is, of course. That's just God's way—and you might as well get used to it.

For Christmas Eve

"God was in Christ reconciling the world to himself,"[97] but it looked like the most normal, natural thing in the world: a baby being born (under something less than optimal conditions). God at work in our lives and in our world often doesn't look miraculous, even though it is. Remember: God doesn't need to impress anyone; He just has to get the job done. And does He ever get the job done!

The angels glorified and praised God because they knew what God was doing for the world. The shepherds glorified and praised God because they heard about what God was doing for them— and then they experienced it—when they responded to the gospel message.

Where are you going for Christmas? There is only one really essential Christmas trip—and all of us need to make it. You need to go to Jesus—Emmanuel—God with us.

> *"To you is born this day*
> *in the city of David* [in Bethlehem]
> *a Savior who is Christ the Lord.*
> *…you will find him*
> *wrapped in swaddling cloths*
> *and lying in a manger…"*

You have heard the good news. Go and see for yourself. And tell.

---

[97] 2 Corinthians 5:19, KJV.

22.

The Christmas Story

Luke 2:1-20 KJV (p. 142)

I'm sure there's no surprise that I would select this passage for Christmas Eve. It is, after all, the passage we think of when we think of the Christmas Story. We may add in the wise men from Matthew, but this is the classic Christmas Story for most people. And it's a great story, with smelly shepherds in a field and angels filling the sky and a little Baby in a manger, surveying His new world. We read it every Christmas. Some of you may know it by heart.

It's a wonderful story—but so what? What is it about this beautiful story that makes it any better—any more important—than some fairy tale you might tell a little child you're tucking in bed for the night?

What makes this story so truly wonderful is not the beauty of the story, but the deeper truth the story conveys. The reason we tell this particular story year after year, century after century, is not the exotic setting or the colorful characters or the mysterious plot. The point and power of the Christmas Story is the simple truth it reveals: God is *for* us.

We noted in past weeks, as we prepared for the coming of Christmas, that the gospel writers pointed to the coming of Jesus

Christ as the proof that God is both *with* us (Emmanuel), and *like* us (Incarnate Word become flesh). The announcement to the shepherds and the celebration of the angels' choir that *"a Savior has been born to you...Christ the Lord"* is important because it shows that God is *for* us. The angel says, *"I bring you good news of great joy that will be for all the people."* That includes you and me and everybody we know.

God is with us. God is like us. God is for us.

Imagine a bunch of ordinary kids shooting baskets on a playground. Then imagine that Michael Jordan himself wanders up out of nowhere to watch them play. Just think what it must feel like to be one of those kids and know that Michael Jordan is with you, right there on your playground. Then imagine that Michael Jordan, all of a sudden, steps out onto that little playground basketball court and starts shooting baskets just like everybody else. He shoots better than everybody else, of course, but there he is, shooting baskets, just like you and your friends. Just think what it must feel like to know that Michael Jordan is doing the same thing you are doing.

And then imagine that Michael Jordan says, "Let's play," and offers to be on your side. Just think what it would feel like if Michael Jordan was playing for your team, on your side. Well, Michael Jordan may be the "king of the court" in basketball, but in life itself he is nothing compared to Messiah Jesus, the King of all Creation. And God has sent Jesus the Messiah, not just to sit in the stands and watch you, not just to run up and down the court like you, but to be on your team, to play the ultimate game for your benefit.

The birth of Jesus is the proof—the ultimate evidence—that God is for us. But to appreciate what this means, you have to remember that it didn't have to be that way. God didn't have to be for us. God doesn't have to be for us now. Can you imagine what it would be like if God were *against* you instead of *for* you? It's not a pretty picture. Listen to the words of Jeremiah, when the people of Jerusalem found themselves on the wrong side of God: *"Thus says the Lord, the God of Israel, '...I myself will fight against you with outstretched hand and strong arm, in anger, and in fury, and in great wrath. And I will smite the inhabitants of this city, both man and beast; they shall die of a great pestilence.'"*[98]

And you may be thinking: that sounds more like what I've been going through.

Maybe this doesn't seem like the greatest Christmas you've even seen. Maybe you haven't been able to find a lot of *"peace on earth, good will toward men"* this year to wrap your Christmas season in.

"If God is for me, He's got a funny way of showing it."

Still, the angel tells the shepherds, *"...a great joy will come to all the people."* God *is* for us. God weighs in—through Jesus—on our side. Of course, sometimes, when it seems that God has lined up against us, He has. Sometimes God lines up against us because we are actually lined up against ourselves. God is for us and we are against ourselves. At those times when we are our own worst enemies, even then, God is for us. James Taylor has a line in one of his love songs that says, "You were better for me than I was for myself."[99] We could sing that just as truthfully to God.

And remember, Jesus was born on the straw of a stable, not on sheets of silk. The news—the good news—was revealed to those smelly shepherds, not to perfumed potentates. And after the smelly shepherds saw the Baby in Bethlehem they had only their sheep, and the fields, and the cold night to go back to. But they went back changed forever, because now they knew: no matter what their world looked like, the Creator of that world was for

---

[98] Jeremiah 21:4-6, RSV.
[99] In checking my references for this book, I discovered that, though the song, "How Sweet It Is (To Be Loved by You)," was recorded by James Taylor in 1975, it was written by Brian Holland and Lamont Dozier in 1964, and first recorded by Marvin Gaye that same year. Working from memory, I also misquoted the line slightly in the sermon. The actual wording is: "You were better *to* me than *I've been* to myself."

them. The birth of Jesus was the greatest gift of all for them because it conveyed to them the greatest news of all: God is for us.

So what is the benefit of this gift that makes it so wonderful for people like us, stuck in our particular life situations this Christmas? Paul asked in Romans, *"If God be for us, who can be against us?"*[100] Paul doesn't mean no one would oppose us. Paul had more opposition than he could keep up with. He means who can *effectively* oppose us. Who can prevent what God is doing in us *ultimately*?

Paul went on to say, *"He who did not spare his own Son but gave him up* **for**— **us**— **all**, *will he not give us all things with him?"*[101] Of course, Paul is not suggesting we should forward our Christmas shopping list to God as though He were some cosmic Santa Claus. Paul saw that God had given all things in eternity to the One born in Bethlehem and crucified at Calvary. And Paul was convinced by what he had seen of God's favor that God would share the eternal gifts of Christ with those who accepted God's gift of this Christ to them, and the sacrifice of this Christ for them.

Let me ask you a question: Will you be leaving any gifts under your tree tomorrow?

Surely some of what we give each other will be the wrong size, or the wrong color, or just "wrong." We'll return a lot of presents next week that just turned out to be wrong. But won't we open *all* of them? Won't we "receive" them, regardless? We won't leave them under the tree.

Well, there's nothing wrong with the Christmas present God has for us. It may lack the fancy wrapping of the things we cram under the tree for each other. But there is nothing wrong—and absolutely everything right—with the gift God has given us, even if it happens to be wrapped in swaddling clothes. God has given us a Savior, a Savior Who is *with* us and *like* us and *for* us.

And it is now our Christmas story. And what an incredibly wonderful story it turns out to be! The Creator and Sustainer of all

---

[100] Romans 8:31, KJV.
[101] Romans 8:32, KJV.

the universe has chosen to be near us and available to us. The transcendent God is with us. The Source of infinite wisdom and power has chosen to empty Himself of these divine attributes and become fully and finitely human. The omnipotent and omniscient God has become like us. The Essence of holiness and righteousness has chosen to provide salvation for the sinful inhabitants of an insignificant world. The redeeming God is for us.

And what role are we to play as the current characters in God's ongoing Christmas story? We may borrow from the shepherds in the original Christmas story: Hear the good news God presents and respond to it in faith. Confirm it for yourself by accepting God's invitation to come and see for yourself. Tell other people what (and especially Who) you have encountered, and then celebrate the miracle God has performed in your life, the miracle that, like so many others, just reconfirms what we've been saying all along: God is with us. God is like us. God is for us.

God bless you. Merry Christmas to you—and for you—all.

23.

The Christmas Story (Abridged)

Luke 2:1-20 KJV (p. 142)

I'm sure there's no surprise that I would select this passage for Christmas Eve. It is, after all, the passage we think of when we think of The Christmas Story. We may add in the wise men from Matthew, but this is the classic Christmas Story for most people. And it's a great story, with smelly shepherds in a field and angels filling the sky and a little Baby in a manger, surveying His new world. We read it every Christmas. Some of you may know it by heart.

It's a wonderful story—but so what? What is it about this beautiful story that makes it any better—any more important—than some fairy tale you might tell a little child you're tucking in bed for the night?

What makes this story so truly wonderful is not the beauty of the story, but the deeper truth the story conveys. The reason we tell this particular story year after year, century after century, is not the exotic setting or the colorful characters or the mysterious plot. The point and power of the Christmas Story is the simple truth it reveals: God is *for* us.

The announcement to the shepherds and the celebration of the angels' choir that *"a Savior has been born to you...Christ the Lord"* shows

The Christmas Story (Abridged)

that God is *for* us. The angel says, *"I bring you good news of great joy that will be for all the people."* That includes you and me and everybody we know.

The birth of Jesus is the proof—the ultimate evidence—that God is for us. But to appreciate what this means, you have to remember that it didn't have to be that way. God didn't have to be for us. Can you imagine what it would be like if God were *against* you instead of *for* you? It's not a pretty picture.

Still, the angel tells the shepherds, *"...a great joy will come to all the people."* God *is* for us. God weighs in—through Jesus—on our side.

And remember, Jesus was born on the straw of a stable, not on sheets of silk. The news—the good news—was revealed to those smelly shepherds, not to perfumed potentates. And after the smelly shepherds saw the Baby in Bethlehem, they had only their sheep, and the fields, and the cold night to go back to. But they went back changed f: no matter what their world looked like, the Creator of that world was *for* them.

Let me ask you a question: Will you be leaving any gifts under your tree tomorrow? Surely some of what we give each other will be the wrong size, or the wrong color, or just "wrong." We'll return a lot of presents next week that just turned out to be "wrong." But won't we open *all* of them? Won't we "receive" them, regardless? We won't leave them under the tree.

Well, there's nothing wrong with the Christmas Present God has for us. There is nothing wrong—and absolutely everything right—with the Gift God has given us, even if It happens to be wrapped in swaddling clothes. God has given us a Savior, a Savior Who is *with* us and *like* us and *for* us.

And it is now our Christmas story. And what an incredibly wonderful story it turns out to be! The Creator and Sustainer of all the universe is with us. The omnipotent and omniscient God has become like us. The holy, righteous and redeeming God is for us—providing salvation for the sinful inhabitants of an insignificant world.

And what role are we to play, as the current characters in God's ongoing Christmas story? We may borrow from the shepherds in the original Christmas story: Hear the good news God presents and respond to it in faith. Confirm it for yourself by accepting God's invitation to come and see for yourself. Tell other people what (and especially Who) you have encountered, and then celebrate the miracle God has performed in your life, the miracle that, like so many others, just reconfirms these remarkable truths of Christmas: God is with us. God is like us. God is for us.

God bless you. Merry Christmas to you—and for you—all.

24.

The Time Came

Luke 2:1-20 KJV (p. 142)

Tonight, we celebrate Christmas. We decorate this holy place with beautiful flowers and light a host of candles. We read the sacred story once again and sing the familiar songs about a little town and a manger bed and a silent, holy night. This is the most wonderful service held in this sanctuary all year.

But all that takes place here tonight in this beautiful church flooded with flowers and glowing with light—all the pageantry of the children in the earlier service and the solemn procession we will make to the communion rail a little later ourselves—all the inspiring music—and even this splendid sermon—are not Christmas.

For that matter, even all the decorations and presents, the good food and gathered family in the homes to which you will go when you leave here—all of these things are not Christmas.

They are merely testimony to Christmas and celebration of it.

Christmas is the birth of a Baby—born like every other baby—even though this Baby was like no baby born before or since—like no other baby who ever came into this world. This Baby was—and is—the Savior of all mankind—the Messiah sent from God.

The Time Came

It is good to celebrate Christmas. It is even better to testify to it. The Bible does both—"with wise men and angels and shepherds and all."[102] But it is important that we do not confuse the celebration with the thing we celebrate. Christmas is the birth of a Baby Who is also God.

About this birth, the Bible is remarkably low-key. The telling of it is simple and straightforward. The Gospel of Matthew says, *"This is how the birth of Jesus Christ came about...[Mary] gave birth to a son. And [Joseph] gave him the name Jesus."*[103]

As you heard earlier, Luke says, *"...the time came for the baby to be born, and [Mary] gave birth to her firstborn, a son."*

Christmas: the birth of a Baby.

But babies are born every day. It's the most natural thing in the world. Every one of us started out that way. And Jesus was born just like everybody else.

But Jesus was different. The birth of Jesus was different because *He* was born in a way that was *not* different from you or me or anyone else, even though, as John points out in the Fourth Gospel, the birth of Jesus means that the eternally preexistent Word Who is God became flesh and made His dwelling among us.

The reason the birth of this particular Baby—among all the babies ever born—is Christmas is that *this* Baby—this Jesus—is the unique One Who came from the Father, and was full of God's grace and truth, God's divinity, even as a Baby—in the moment of His birth.[104] It means all that, but Luke just says, *"the time came for the baby to be born"*—and He was.

The testimony and the celebration will come later; angels will appear in the sky and tell the news and celebrate. Shepherds will rush down to the village to see the Baby and celebrate and tell others what they have seen. Later, wise men will follow a star and

---

[102] From the hymn, "I Wonder as I Wander," by John Jacob Niles, 1933.
[103] Matthew 1:18-25, NIV.
[104] John 1:1-18.

bring gifts to this Christmas Child[105] and start the whole Christmas shopping season.

But none of that is Christmas. Christmas is: *"The time came for the Baby to be born, and she gave birth..."*

Christmas. Birth of this one particular Baby. It's that simple.

But not really. The simplicity of its telling doesn't begin to tell the story. Christmas is the birth of this Baby. But it didn't start there, and it doesn't end there. Or we wouldn't be here, tonight.

Luke doesn't just say that *"the Baby was born."* He says, ***"the time came** for the Baby to be born."* Luke is writing, on the surface, about nine months—give or take a few days. The focus of the actual words is more on the mother's pregnancy than the Baby's birth.

Older translations say, *"...the days were completed for her to give birth."*

Luke writes words about a normal human birth at the end of a normal human pregnancy.

But what he means is something entirely different. Several weeks ago, I talked about the difference between man's time and God's time.

Luke describes Christmas—the birth of this Baby—Jesus—in man's time. But it took place in both. On a particular day in the history of mankind, while every person living on earth was doing something, the time came for this particular Baby to be born.

The rulers of the great empires of the day were enjoying the perks of their power. The administrators under their authority were ensuring a steady stream of revenue for the government and its officials. Individuals were responding to the heavy hand of government upon their pocketbooks, in some cases by going to distant towns to get their names on census rolls that would qualify them and their children for lower taxes.

---

[105] Matthew 2:1-12.

The Time Came

Two of the individuals caught up in these events and going about their business were a man named Joseph, and Mary, the woman he had recently married.

"While they were there," Luke says—while they were doing what life required of them at the moment—as life requires of everyone, including us—*"the time came for the Baby to be born."* That's what happened in their time, and we celebrate it and testify to it, in our time.

But we and they and everybody else also exist in God's time. In God's time, Christmas began thousands of years before a Child was conceived in Mary's womb, when a holy and righteous God decided not to destroy the sinful humanity He loves, but to redeem us instead.

And all the angels of heaven have rejoiced in heaven throughout all the time of man, knowing what man did not know about what God was going to do—when the time came. In God's time, the birth of this Baby came not merely at the end of a nine-month biological process, but at the culmination of God's raising up and reducing nations and His leading a people of His own choosing through centuries of captivity and deliverance in accordance with covenants He established to prepare them for the time when this Baby would be born.

In God's time, Christmas did not merely come one night in Bethlehem and slip immediately into history, as all events in man's time do. In God's time, the time is always coming for this Baby to be born to men and women who have not experienced Christmas, no matter how many Christmases they have celebrated. In God's time, the time comes for this Baby—Jesus Christ, the Savior, the Messiah, God Himself—to be born into the lives of people while they are doing whatever it is they're doing and thinking whatever they are thinking in this life they are living.

In our time, the minutes are ticking away till midnight and the beginning of a new day on the calendar that has "Christmas" written across it. In God's time, Christmas is whenever Jesus is born into your life and becomes the real presence of God to you—day or night, summer or winter, early or late in the passage of your human years, while whatever else is going on in the course of your human time.

For me, the time came for the Baby to be born on a Monday night at the end of a revival meeting in the church my family had attended since before I was born. As I responded to an invitation from a visiting preacher—who spoke a lot longer and louder than I have tonight—Christ the Savior was born in me. That was my Christmas.

Since then, it has all been celebration—and a bit of testimonial, too, so that others who have never experienced Christmas itself might discover that the time has come for the Baby to be born to them and in them.

Christmas celebrations can be wonderful, with lights and colors and beautiful displays, with presents and parties and tidings of joy. But no celebration can match the wonder and the glory and the power of the thing celebrated. *"...the time came for the Baby to be born, and she gave birth to a Son."* That's Christmas.

And when the time comes for this Baby, this Jesus, to be born in you, that is God's Christmas for you:

"For unto you is born...
a Savior Who is Christ the Lord."

25.

Come Closer

Luke 2:1-20 KJV (p. 142)

You know the story by heart—this Christmas story. You've heard it or read it dozens of times. You've sung or listened to hundreds of carols about it—seen thousands of pictures depicting the shepherds in the field and the birth of Jesus in Bethlehem. It has a certain romance about it—a bit of simple, captivating charm—staying power.

There's Bethlehem, the city of David. (It was just a village, really, not as big as our little town). But David was born there, the shepherd boy who grew up to become a king—the greatest king of Israel. David was "a thousand years ago" for Luke and those who first read this story. That's a lot of nights and a lot of shepherds sitting out in the field, like David, looking after the sheep.

The shepherds in the story had spent too many nights to count in that very field outside Bethlehem. But this was the first time heaven ever opened up—the first time angels ever proclaimed the birth of a Baby—back there in town—in their Bethlehem.

But on this night, Bethlehem produced another David—another Shepherd King—another Leader to gather the human sheep of God's flock. Here was a night like every other night, and then, it was like no other night these shepherds had ever known—

like no night ever experienced by a hundred generations of shepherds before them in any of those grazing fields around Bethlehem. It was all new and completely unexpected to the shepherds.

We, on the other hand, come out to join the shepherds every year, knowing the angels will come, just as they did last year and have every year since that first year. We already know what the shepherds are going to find in the village. We know the story.

We know Mary and Joseph have finally made it to Bethlehem and found a place to stay—however makeshift. We know the Baby has been born. We know what the shepherds are going to see and hear out there in the night and what they're going to do about it—where they're going to go.

The Bethlehem shepherds, out in the cold and dark, were told about the birth of a Messiah. Did you know they had been praying for the birth of a Messiah—THE Messiah—all their lives, just like their ancestors and all of Israel had been doing for centuries? And on this night, the Messiah—their Messiah—is born. This Baby is what all Israel had been waiting for—and what you and I and every other person on earth have been waiting for, too—all our lives—whether we knew it or not.

"Unto you is born..." You know, when somebody says, "Oh look: it's a new baby!" most people take a look. The shepherds look up and see an angel saying, "Look! There's a new Baby in Bethlehem." So they naturally want to go look.

So the shepherds go—to have a look for themselves. You could let others go, and then let them tell you what they saw. But it's not the same as going and seeing for yourself. You really need to see for yourself.

The shepherds go to see this Baby. You know the story. The shepherds go, and you naturally go with them. But how do you go? And how close do you go to this manger scene you know so well? Where do you stand when you and the shepherds come and see the Messiah—the Savior—the Christmas Baby?

For Christmas Eve

You come here—to the Christmas scene—every year. You know the story by heart. Do you just give the Baby a glance—hang around on the edge of the crowd—maybe hop up on your tiptoes from time to time? Is it "old hat?" Do you just glance over now, like driving by the crèche outside? Yes, you will see something that way. You can say you've "seen the Baby." You can "check the block."

After all, if you come into Bethlehem with the shepherds again and look, what are you going to see? A baby. A normal baby. A baby like all the other babies you've ever seen. A baby dressed up in the kind of clothes babies are normally dressed up in. Clothes like you put on babies at your house. Nothing special.

Of course, a baby in a manger is different—even shepherds don't usually put their babies where the animals eat. And you certainly don't expect to see a Savior Messiah in a rustic, makeshift nursery, even as a baby. You would expect royal robes and golden cribs.

The truth is, you wouldn't know there was anything special or important about this Baby unless you had been told He's special and important by some special and important messengers. Those messengers—those angels—say this Son of David will make all the accomplishments of David—and of all the descendants of David who followed him—seem like child's play by comparison. But you wouldn't know it to look at Him now, this normal-looking Baby, lying there in the manger.

It's a newborn Baby, after all. It—He—can't do anything yet. For now, the little Baby just seems human: needing help for the most basic, most important thing—needing someone to nurture Him and keep Him alive.

But one day the roles will be reversed—He will be the One helping all of humanity and nurturing men and women and giving life—in Bethlehem and around the world. But for now, the question is, "What will those who see this Baby do with Him?"

The critical, the unconcerned and the merely curious will naturally hold back. They don't really care to come and see this particular Baby—to get a clear picture of Who—and What—they're dealing with. They already know all they want to know—all they think they need to know. They've seen too much—know too much—understand too much. Or think they do.

You'll need to step out of that crowd and ignore whatever they say about this Baby, if you're going to really see Him. If you're going to see what's so special about Him—what makes Him unique—you're going to have to come closer.

What will happen if you come closer to this Baby? If you come closer, you might go from being a stranger to being an acquaintance—or from an acquaintance to a friend.

You might, by coming closer, actually become a member of the family. By coming all the way up to the manger, you might become related, by blood, to this seemingly average, absolutely unparalleled Child.

You come to Bethlehem every year. You come with the shepherds out of the field and into the presence of this Baby every Christmas. Will you come closer this year? This year, will you come closer to the manger and the holy One it holds? Will you get to know Him better and stay with Him even after this day passes and the shepherds go away? Will you stay with the Christmas Baby?

Don't come and go. Don't come as you always have. Don't merely repeat the experience—warm and pleasing as it may have been. Don't settle for another perfunctory and predictable pilgrimage to the stall in the stable.

This year, this Christmas, come closer. Come closer and stay longer. See more clearly and understand more fully.

Soon, this Bethlehem Baby will leave the manger and Bethlehem—and infancy, for that matter. Will you stay with Him, close to Him?

Where is He going? Oh, to the Temple[106] and to Egypt,[107] to Nazareth[108] and Capernaum,[109] to Jerusalem[110] and Gethsemane,[111] and the Cross[112] and the grave[113]—and to the right hand of the Father in heaven.[114]

Where is He going? "Come and see," He told a man who saw Him and wanted a closer look.[115] "Come and see," said the Bethlehem Baby grown into a Man. But to see Him better, in a crib or on a Cross, you have to come closer to Him.

You cannot come closer to Jesus if you do not move—if you do not change. You cannot do what you have always done and get any closer to Him.

But change?

How?

Move?

Where?

To come closer to Jesus, focus your attention on Him. Look at Him more and study Him more—more closely and more carefully. To come closer to Jesus, come closer to His Word. The more you read and study the Bible, the closer you'll get to Jesus. The more you pray—the more you spend time in conversation with Him—the better you will know Him.

The more you invest yourself in moving closer to Jesus, the closer you will be. The more you want to know Him—the more He will honor and bless your effort and desire with success. Come in from the periphery where people just glance at Jesus from time to time. The closer you come into the center of His "family circle,"

---

[106] Luke 2:22.
[107] Matthew 2:13-14.
[108] Matthew 2:19-23.
[109] Matthew 4:13.
[110] Mark 11:15.
[111] Matthew 26:36.
[112] John 19:17.
[113] Mark 15:46.
[114] Hebrews 1:3.
[115] John 1:36-39.

the more intimate will be your relationship with this Christmas Child—and the more pronounced the family resemblance between you.

Come closer, this Christmas, to this Baby born in Bethlehem—this son of David; this Savior King. Come closer to this humble Child; this holy Christ—this lowly Infant; this Lord of lords.

Come.

Closer.

Christmas Day

26.

The Most Natural Thing in the World

Luke 2:1-20 KJV (p. 142)

Every day, over 10 thousand babies are born in the United States of America.[116] More than a third of a million are born worldwide—every day.[117] The birth of babies is the most natural thing in the world.

Christmas Day will be no different. Babies will be born this Christmas. They always have been, every Christmas. Even in Bethlehem on that first Christmas, at least one baby was born. In fact, the reason it was Christmas was because of a Baby Who was born there.

The angels came later—and the shepherds. The wise men and the star were "follow-up"—"reaction." Before all the hoopla and excitement, there was simply the birth of a Baby—the most natural thing in the world. Luke wrote: *"The days were accomplished that she should be delivered. And she brought forth her firstborn Son...."* Happens all the time.

---

[116] National Center for Health Statistics, located on the Internet at http://www.cdc.gov/nchs/fastats/births.htm.
[117] UNICEF, http://www.theworldcounts.com/stories/How-Many-Babies-Are-Born-Each-Day.

The Most Natural Thing in the World

The birth of a baby is so natural that it can happen far from home, in less than adequate surroundings, without competent medical support, at extremely inconvenient times. Babies are born when the time comes, regardless of the circumstances or situation—whenever, wherever, however. You see that in the story of the birth of Jesus. There's not much to say: He was born just like everybody else: the most natural thing in the world.

And if the angels hadn't shown up—if the special star hadn't gotten somebody's attention—who would have known that a Baby was born in a stable in a town known as Bethlehem? Who would have known—beside the two people who were there when two became three?

Yes, one of them had a dream telling him to claim the Baby. The other had a vision telling her the Baby was coming and she would carry It and give birth to It. Every mother thinks her baby is special, and this mother had better reason than most, but babies are born all the time. Who's going to notice one more? What's another baby?

☙❧

But what about Saviors of the world? Saviors don't come along nearly as often as you might think—certainly not as often as "would-be Saviors" would have you think. Saviors are so special that you would expect them to show up in spectacular ways: chariots of fire, for instance, accompanied by earthquakes, lightning and dreadful omens—cosmic turmoil and epic events.

Saviors of any kind are rare, but genuine Saviors of the world are so rare that, off the top of my head, I can only think of One. Caesar Augustus, of course, claimed to be "the Savior of the World" at the time Jesus was born, but subsequent events soon proved Caesar's claim to be unfounded.

The only verified Savior of the world I know of is the God Who created the world in the first place. The Creator of the world is the One Who decided what "natural" would be. He created nature—all of it—including you and me. He's the One Who decided that the birth of a baby would be the most natural thing in the world.

And then the Savior of the world decided that His coming to save the world would itself be the most natural thing in the world: The Savior of the world—the God of all Creation—the Master and Sustainer of nature itself—became human—became the subject of the most natural thing in the world. God set aside His divine glory and splendor, shed His omniscience and omnipotence, left behind His heavenly authority, to spend the normal nine months growing in the womb of a woman until the most natural thing in the world happened:[118] Unto us *"was born ... a Savior Who was Christ the Lord"*—also known as "God with us."

Luke said simply: "A pregnant woman gave birth." John said, *"The Word—*who was God—*became flesh and dwelled among us."*[119] The birth of a baby is the most natural thing in the world, and yet: that the Baby born in Bethlehem would be God Himself, (as the biblical writers, and Christians worldwide, claim) encompassed in human form, would not, at first blush, count as a natural event.

And so the question: Can it be, that something as natural as the birth of a baby could be, at the same time, the most miraculous and supernatural occurrence in the whole history of nature?

Wonderful, if it is, because there appears to be another most natural thing in the world: sin, the doing of bad things—wrong things—or, for that matter, the thinking of bad things—the wanting of bad things.

Everybody is born, and everybody sins. It's not just "that other guy"—it's you and me, too. There are infinitely more sins than births taking place every day—and you know how many births there are now. It takes nine months to bring a baby to birth and only a split second to give birth to a sin. And the second sin can

---

[118] Philippians 2:6-7.
[119] John 1:14, RSV.

follow the first about that quick, if you're not careful, and sometimes, even when you are.

Maybe sin is the most natural thing in the world.

Or maybe it isn't, if the God Who created everything that exists in His natural order didn't create sin. And the Bible says He didn't.

Can something be the most common thing in the world without being the most natural?

Perhaps.

Perhaps sin is the most un-natural thing in the world because it is the opposite of what God intended when He brought nature into existence, and set it in motion, and told man and woman to be fruitful, and multiply and have dominion—over nature.[120] The birth of babies is natural; the epidemic of sin is not.

So what are we going to do?

Sin is an epidemic without a natural cure. It is so common that no one in this world can overcome it. And so the most natural thing in the world for those who have been born into this world is to desire to be reborn—without the sin—to be able to start over—to get it right for a change. Don't you wish that you could be plucked out of the seamy swamp of sin and start over with a clean slate—and to have that slate wiped clean every time there is a bad mark against you recorded on it? It's the most natural thing in the world to want that.

But what would it take to get rid of a world of sin—and keep the world? You would think something that spectacular—that marvelous—that miraculous—would require the most un-natural—the most super-natural—activity possible.

But, in fact, the most miraculous thing in the world has been "packaged" in the most natural thing in the world. A Baby was born in a stable, of all places, in an out of the way Jewish village, of all places, in a land under foreign domination, of all places, to overcome the sin of the whole natural or un-natural world by

---

[120] Genesis 1:28.

For Christmas Day

infusing all the natural world with the power and grace of the God Who rules both the natural and supernatural realms.

When I was a boy, I would often run out of the house, throwing open the door in front of me and ignoring what happened to it once I was through it. My mother would catch me up short with the call, "Were you born in a barn?!"

This was the woman who bore me. You would think she would know the answer better than I. For the longest time, I would come back in response to her call, close the door and confess that, in fact, to the best of my knowledge, I had not been born in a barn.

I was not born in a barn, by the way. But my Savior was. And my "best knowledge" tells me—not because I figured it out for myself, but because God's word tells me so—that His being born in a barn—in the natural, human way—means that I may be reborn in that Bethlehem barn with Him, not merely by adoring the Baby just born, but by believing that the birth of that baby Boy is somehow also the birth of God as Savior of the world—my world—the world of my sin.

It is the most natural thing in the world for a baby to be born. Now, because a Child was born in Bethlehem Who was also God, you and I can go to that stable and be born again—because of Him, in Him, by Him. Where once we had to wait for something like the fiery chariots, the cosmic storms and omens of dubious value to bring our Savior—the Savior of our world—to us and our desperate need, now we know that the most supernatural miracle in the whole business is the completely natural way God chose to meet the need of mankind.

God has made it possible, as the early liturgy puts it, "by His one oblation of Himself once offered"[121]—on the Cross, certainly, but first in a stable, or before that even, in a womb—for our new birth—our salvation—which once was humanly impossible—to become the most natural thing in the world.

---

[121] From *The Episcopal Book of Common Prayer,* 1928.

And now, understanding *that*, let us invite the choirs of angels and celebrating shepherds and worshipping wise men back into the picture to point to the importance of what took place without fanfare in the ignored seclusion of a stable stall. Knowing what God was doing in Bethlehem through the birth of Jesus makes our joy and our wonder, our submission and faith, the most natural thing— not just in our world—but throughout all God's supernatural realm.

So come, let us adore Him—"with angels and archangels and all the company of heaven"[122]—and all the redeemed on earth. Come, let us adore Him: Christ the Lord—the God Who was born a Man to become the Savior of the world.

Knowing what we know, adoring the Baby born in Bethlehem and believing in Him as the divine Savior of the world—our world—is the most natural thing in the world.

---

[122] From *The Episcopal Book of Common Prayer*, 1928.

27.

Born Today

Luke 2:1-20 KJV (p. 142)

On this day, many years ago, the sun rose over the Judean hills and light came to the little town of Bethlehem. The town lay in stillness as morning broke upon it, despite the commotion of the night before. A Child had been born in the wee hours of darkness—a Boy—and though the birth of babies is not uncommon, the circumstances surrounding this birth were.

And before all was said and done, more than a few people had found their sleep disturbed, some by the first cries of the Baby, more by the clamoring of shepherds who came in from the fields looking for the Baby, and then by their rowdy ruckus when they had found Him. The shepherds had talked and acted like the birth of this Baby was the greatest thing in the world. It had been quite a night for a little town like Bethlehem.

☙❧

But now, the shepherds are gone, and the townsfolk are catching up on their lost sleep.

The new mother and her Child are resting, too. The Baby, snug in the cloths His mother has wrapped around Him, is napping in a makeshift cradle before His next feeding. The mother, lying physically exhausted near her Newborn, is nonetheless deep in fascinated thought at this latest in a series of exceptional events she has experienced as a result of carrying this Child.

What had the shepherds said? They had seen and heard an angel? Was it *her* angel?

What did they hear? *"...born this day...a Savior Who is Messiah and Lord!"* A sign given and seen. Amazing!

❦

On this day, several hours ago, the sun rose over *our* little town, and though all is calm in the stillness of the morning, we, like the unnamed, unknown shepherds and citizens of Bethlehem, are told of the birth of a Savior and invited to come and see.

"Been there—done that"? Lived through a few Christmases—or more than a few? Know all about the birth of Jesus, do you? Has familiarity faded the fascination?

Too bad. Like the angel, all I can do is *"bring you good news of great joy."* I can tell you about a Savior born to you—born today—but you must decide to come and see.

The Bible tells us about the first Christmas: the day a Savior is born to a virgin mother in a Bethlehem stable—and an angel tells shepherds nearby that this Savior is born to them, too—with divine glory in the sky and in the praise of all heaven's angels, just because it's Christmas.

And Mary, and perhaps the shepherds, too, are changed forever because this Child has been born and they have seen that It has, and whether they understand exactly what it means or not, they believe it means what the angel says it means—for them: *salvation*—salvation from everything they want to be saved from—and everything they need to be saved from, whether they want to be or not.

But what you need to understand is that this is just the first Christmas—the first time Jesus is born—the first time the Savior comes to individuals who are told what is happening and see it happening for themselves.

In fact, there are many Christmases in the Bible. There is a Christmas at the Jordan River where John the Baptist is the divine messenger: *"Behold, the Lamb of God, who takes away the sins of the world."* [123] And for those who go and see and believe—it's Christmas.

There is a Christmas along the seaside in Galilee when fishermen see Jesus and leave their nets[124]—the way the shepherds left their flocks—to see if what they were told about this Savior is true. And they see that it is.

Christmas came on the Damascus Road when the persecutor Paul saw so much Jesus he couldn't see anything else.[125] And when he could see again, all he wanted to see was Jesus.

And then there was *your* first Christmas—that day when you decided to see if what you had been told about God giving a Savior was true—that day when a Savior, Christ the Lord, was born to you—the day that you dropped whatever you were doing to go and see Jesus, and did see Him, and believed that He was born for you—to be your Savior. That, for you, was Christmas, as much or more than the Christmas in Bethlehem Luke recorded.

And so we celebrate *this* Christmas, together as a body of believers on *this* day, because the Christmas that came about on *this* day—the birth of Jesus in Bethlehem—made possible all our individual, personal Christmas Days. We celebrate the birth of Jesus in Bethlehem because we have experienced the birth of Jesus in our own hearts and lives.

We celebrate the birth of Jesus on this day knowing that there is not a day on the calendar that is *not* Christmas Day for someone—some Christian who came to see—and received the salvation of the Savior born to him or her. From January 1st to

---

[123] John 1:29, RSV.
[124] Mark 1:16-20.
[125] Acts 9:1-9.

Born Today

December 31st, every day has been the birthday of the Savior Christ the Lord for someone—every day for almost 2,000 years.

This morning, the sun rose on another Christmas Day. And we celebrate the birth of the Messiah in the stillness of this hour. But soon—all too soon—we will leave this holy time and place, and go back out into the world. In a few days, the "Christmas season" will be over. The world will get back to business as usual. Decorations will come down. Trees will go out to the curb. The kids will have broken or become bored with most of their Christmas toys. The calendar's Christmas will have come and gone.

But you need to realize that just as every day for centuries has been Christmas Day for someone, so every day to come—every day till Jesus returns—will be Christmas Day for others.

Today and every day for as long as there are days, someone in this world will come to Jesus and see, as he or she has been told, that the Baby born in Bethlehem is indeed the Savior God has sent. Every day, there will be people who come to find Jesus—and they will find that Jesus has been born into their hearts. Every day will be Christmas for someone, just as there was a day—a Christmas—when Jesus was born to us.

❧❦

On that first Christmas, after a messenger of God had told some unlikely souls about the birth of the Savior, all of heaven's angels burst into song, praising God for what He had done and celebrating the benefit to all mankind. It is not inconceivable that heaven's angels burst into that same song every time someone experiences Christmas. What better service could they render to God than to praise His goodness and power in giving us a Savior, or to reflect His joy when even one of His children accepts His gift?

But though an angel announced to Mary that she would give birth to God's Messiah, and an angel later shared with the shepherds that the Baby was born, God's "Christmas messenger service" has been expanded. As the angel told the shepherds, the shepherds, having discovered the truth for themselves, told others. Every person who has experienced Christmas—every person within whom the Savior has been born and dwells—is now the capable messenger called by God to announce the *"good news of great joy"* that has been, and will be, for all people.

Eloquence is not required. Theological credentials may prove counter-productive.

The Christmas message is simple and goes something like this: "Hey! Great news! There is a Savior from God for *you*! Come and see for yourself what I'm telling you. If you come, you will see. And when you see that what I am telling you is true, the Savior will be born in you. And you will experience your own personal Christmas. And all the angels of heaven will sing '*Glory!*' because you will have believed and accepted what God has done for you."

On that remarkable, unique night in Bethlehem, a Baby was born, and shepherds showed up to see Him, and they acted like the birth of this Baby was the greatest thing in the world.

Turns out they were right. It was Christmas, and it has been ever since—for those of us who have come to Jesus. It was Christmas, and it will be Christmas, today or any day, when you let this Savior be born in you.

Unto Us a Son is Given

Isaiah 9:2, 6-7 KJV

² The people that walked in darkness have seen a great light: they that dwell in the land of the shadow of death, upon them hath the light shined.

⁶ For unto us a child is born, unto us a son is given: and the government shall be upon his shoulder: and his name shall be called Wonderful, Counsellor, The mighty God, The everlasting Father, The Prince of Peace.

⁷ Of the increase of his government and peace there shall be no end, upon the throne of David, and upon his kingdom, to order it, and to establish it with judgment and with justice from henceforth even for ever. The zeal of the LORD *of hosts will perform this.*

28.

Unto Us a Son is Given

Isaiah 9:2, 6-7; Luke 2:1-20 KJV (p. 142)

In our modern, scientific age, we know so much more about just about everything than those who lived hundreds and thousands of years before us knew. They knew the sun rose in the east and set in the west each day. We know that the earth revolves around the sun, which seems to rise and set because the earth rotates on its own axis every 24 hours. They knew that seasons come and go, year by year, each at its appointed time and always in due sequence. We know the ebb and flow of the seasons reflects the pendulum-like movement of the poles of the earth as our planet makes its annual orbit around the sun. They knew they were a people walking in darkness who needed a great light. We know...

Perhaps the people living in this modern, scientific age don't know so much more about everything after all.

The "light" that Isaiah and others were looking for was not the kind that comes from the sun in the sky, but the kind that came from the coming of a royal son—a person born to a ruler who would rule one day in a way that would bless all those who lived their lives under that rule.

And because that didn't *have* to happen—unlike the rising and setting of the sun and the passing parade of the seasons—on those infrequent occasions when it *did* happen—when a royal son *was* born—ancient people recognized it as the glorious gift of God that it was. Anarchy might be averted for another generation. Order might operate during the lifetime of the new prince. It was enough to say, *"Unto us a child is born; unto us a son is given,"* to give God's people hope. There was now a chance to live in the light instead of darkness.

Yes, for all we know in our modern, scientific age, there are some remarkably important things some people do not seem to know these days.

Look how many times the history of the salvation of the world hinges on God's gift of a son. After sin entered the world and Adam and Eve were ejected from the Garden,[126] Eve acknowledged the gift of a son from God, the sign that God would perpetuate the human race, in spite of the sin that perverted His divine image within us.[127] That first son, Cain, grew up to murder his brother, Abel, and make himself the epitome of "the lost soul." And yet, when he did, God gave this first family another son, Seth, through whom God began to work out the redemption Cain and all the other sinful sons and daughters of mankind who followed him would require.

God promised a son to Abraham and Sarah in their laughably old age, and gave them, eventually, not the son they connived to conceive through a concubine, but the son God promised them—the special son, Isaac—through whom alone God would fulfill His greater promise of place and protection, power and prominence to the nation that would descend from Abraham across the centuries to come.[128]

And out of the two sons of Isaac, God gave one, Jacob, to be the son of promise.[129] And out of the twelve sons of Jacob, one—

---

[126] Genesis 3.
[127] Genesis 4—5.
[128] Genesis 12—25.
[129] Genesis 25—33.

Joseph—would fulfill God's promise of salvation in the short term, by feeding his family in Egypt, while another—Judah—would carry the divine promise into the distant future, through a descendant's seventh son named David, who went from shepherd boy to shepherd king.[130]

And God gave David a son, Solomon, who, despite his father's sin, rose to rule over God's people with unrivaled splendor[131]—and more importantly—perpetuated a line of sons that would, centuries later—after the rise and fall of many descendants—produce a latter-day son of David who would one day lead his pregnant wife into the sanctuary of a stable in the town where David was born.[132]

And the One to be born in that stable—then wrapped in swaddling clothes and bedded down in manger straw—would turn out to be God's ultimate gift of a Son. The One born in that stable would be a son of Joseph—and, therefore, a son of David, and, therefore, a son of Abraham, and, therefore, a son of Adam.

But the One born in the Bethlehem stable would also be the ultimate gift of a Son because He alone—of every son who ever lived—was also the only-begotten Son of God. God had finally—in the fullness of time—given us a Son Who really was—and would be for us—the Light of the world. God gave us a Son Who would be the greatest Light ever to appear upon this sin-darkened earth—because this particular divine Son had already been the Light of heaven even before there was a Creation—and the Light of all Creation from the very instant He brought all other light into existence.

---

[130] Genesis 37—50; 1 Samuel 16; 2 Samuel 5.
[131] 2 Samuel 11—12; 1 Kings 1—2, 10.
[132] Matthew 1; Luke 2.

In our modern, scientific age, we know—with modern, scientific certainty—*when* the universe came into being and *how* it happened.

But we cannot determine—by our modern, scientific ways—*why* it happened—and *Who made* it happen. For those answers, you have to go back to the ancient wisdom conveyed to us modern folk in the timeless words of revelation. And the same is true if you are to appreciate the purpose and power of the Son given to us in that faraway place in that faraway time.

Many in our country are currently fixated on a cadre of men and women who want us to put our government upon their shoulders. Each would have us believe that he or she is perceptive, powerful, persevering and the best at making and maintaining peace. They would have us believe that the benefit of giving the government to them would be immeasurable.

But none of them can transform a land of deep darkness into one of great light. Only one Person can do that: the Son God has given us. That's what this unique and sacred Son was given to us for.

Look at what He has done since God gave Him to us: *"...the blind receive their sight and the lame walk, lepers are cleansed and the deaf hear, and the dead are raised up, and the poor have good news preached to them."*[133]

This is, I admit, in the language of sacred scripture. But let's put it in our own words: Jesus grew up from His birth in Bethlehem to a manhood devoted to divine miracles wherever He went. Laid with love in a rough wooden cradle as a Baby—He would be hammered with hate onto a rough wooden Cross as a Man and die to deter the course of divine justice away from the condemnation all sinners deserve.

And through the ages since—even into our modern, scientific age—every person who has accepted the gift of this Son given by

---

[133] Matthew 11:5.

God Himself has been brought out of sin's darkness into God's light. Every person who has seen this Son's light has become a child of God, a child born to God because we know that Jesus is the Son of God given to us.

So many people in our modern, scientific age know this cannot be so. So many people know the earth revolves around the sun and rotates upon its axis, but do not know—in fact, refuse to know—that there is a God behind all they know, Who has given us His Son, Who alone is able to overcome the darkness in our world and in our hearts, just as His countless stars overcome the darkness of the universe—a darkness that would be complete without the light He called into being when He chose to call all things—including us—into being.

Today, we hear again the ancient words—the timeless, revealed truth of the God Who is not impressed with what our modern, scientific age claims to know about what is and what is not. Today, we rejoice that God's Son has been given to us—the goal of God's giving all those other sons—and daughters—throughout the pageant of His saving history.

God has put the government—of this world and all worlds—on the shoulders of this Son, because God wants us to live in the light of life and eternity, and not in the darkness. And God has given the Son (that He has given us) the ability to exercise for us—and demonstrate to us—God's infinite wisdom and power, God's unending love and provision, God's unassailable authority and aptitude to bring peace and harmony into every aspect of His Creation.

Can a newborn baby do all this?

Only if He is the Child born to us—the Son given to us—by God. Only if this Baby in Bethlehem this Christmas Day is the fulfillment of Isaiah's prophecy and God's promise made early and often throughout the ages.

Nothing else we know in our modern, scientific age is worth knowing, if we don't know that. And if we do know that, we know all we'll ever need to know—now and for all the ages to come.

Isaiah said, *"Unto you a child is born..."* The angel said, *"...unto you is born this day in the city of David, a Savior, Who is Christ the Lord."*

Now, you know.

29.

In the Flesh

John 1:1-14 NRSV

¹ In the beginning was the Word, and the Word was with God, and the Word was God. ² He was in the beginning with God. ³ All things came into being through him, and without him not one thing came into being. What has come into being ⁴ in him was life, and the life was the light of all people. ⁵ The light shines in the darkness, and the darkness did not overcome it.

⁶ There was a man sent from God, whose name was John. ⁷ He came as a witness to testify to the light, so that all might believe through him. ⁸ He himself was not the light, but he came to testify to the light. ⁹ The true light, which enlightens everyone, was coming into the world.

¹⁰ He was in the world, and the world came into being through him; yet the world did not know him. ¹¹ He came to what was his own, and his own people did not accept him. ¹² But to all who received him, who believed in his name, he gave power to become children of God, ¹³ who were born, not of blood or of the will of the flesh or of the will of man, but of God.

¹⁴ And the Word became flesh and lived among us, and we have seen his glory, the glory as of a father's only son, full of grace and truth.

৵•৻

Last night, as darkness fell and Christmas began, the Chapel filled up with people. They came to hear the familiar story and sing the well-known carols. It was a boisterous crowd: little boys squirmed in the pews and babies fussed in their mother's arms as the temperature and humidity rose a little too high for comfort. The people heard and sang about angels and shepherds, wise men and shining stars, and about a Baby born to a set of parents in a very difficult set of circumstances.

But the highlight of the evening was the parade of angels and shepherds and wise men, coming right down our center aisle to gather around our Mary and Joseph and baby Jesus. Our children and grandchildren created a live nativity scene as the centerpiece of our Christmas worship.

Now, our "angels" were smaller (probably) than the heavenly host singing *"Glory to God"* that first Christmas. Our "shepherds" had little-to-no actual experience tending sheep, I suspect. Our "wise men" are still in school. But with their help, *there* was the Christmas story—in the *flesh*.

And now, in the clear light of Christmas morning, we read, not the familiar story with its colorful characters and dramatic action, but the mature and measured analysis of what the story means.

"Now the birth of Jesus Christ took place in this way," says Matthew.[134] There were dreams with divine messages and disasters narrowly avoided, and Jesus was born in Bethlehem of Judea in the days of Herod the King.

But John goes back much farther than that. John says, *"In the beginning was the Word, and the Word was with God, and the Word was God."*

☙❧

"[T]he angel Gabriel was sent from God to a city of Galilee named Nazareth," says Luke.[135] And the angel told the Virgin Mary she would conceive and bear a son named Jesus. And in the process, there would be choirs of angels singing and a flock of shepherds

---

[134] Matthew 1:18, RSV.
[135] Luke 1:26, RSV.

For Christmas Day

wandering in to have a look at a Baby born in a barn and sleeping on straw.

And, about all this, John says only, *"The Word became flesh and lived among us, and we have seen his glory."*

ಹ⊷ॐ

Matthew and Luke tell us the story of the birth of Jesus, and it's a good story, a very human story, which is the point in the end, as John points out. The Word, the power of God present at and producing Creation itself, is now present in that Creation—in the flesh—in our world and in our lives and in our eternal destinies. God has come in the flesh—here—to us—to be a part of us and what we're going through, to know it and experience it from birth to death, from cradle (or manger) to grave (or tomb).

"The Word became flesh"—in humble surroundings with humble witnesses. *"The Word became flesh"* despite the best efforts of Satan to prevent it and Herod to abort it after the fact. *"The Word became flesh...."* God became human in the human way.

John may sound a little too theoretical—a little too ethereal for our purposes. But he ends up in the same place as his gospel-writing colleagues: God—in the flesh. Matthew and Luke tell us the Christmas story. They tell us how Jesus was born.

And John tells us why it matters. John says that this Baby, born on this day, in this town, in this stable, to this mother, is the Grace of the merciful God and the Truth of the righteous God and the Glory of the infinite God—"now in flesh appearing."[136]

Until God came in the flesh, we were in the flesh by ourselves. We were sinful, broken, helpless and hopeless—in the flesh. And Paul summed up our dilemma nicely: *"...flesh and blood cannot inherit the kingdom of God...."*[137]

---

[136] From the hymn, "O Come, All Ye Faithful," a Latin carol whose English version was provided by Frederick Oakeley in 1841.
[137] 1 Corinthians 15:50, NIV.

In the Flesh

But now—today—everything has changed. *"...as the children have partaken of flesh and blood,"* says the writer of Hebrews, *"[Jesus] himself likewise shared in the same, that through death he might destroy him who had the power of death, that is, the devil, and release those who ... were ... subject to bondage."*[138]

"Come to Bethlehem and see
Him Whose birth the angels sing."[139]

What are you coming to see? A pretty baby? Maybe. We don't know and it doesn't matter. How about the eternal, divine Word Who is from God and is God become flesh and dwelling with us? Yes. Yes as announced by the angels and seen by the shepherds and worshipped by the wise men. The baby Jesus—God in the flesh—like you and me—with you and me—to redeem you and me—and render us acceptable to God.

"Come adore on bended knee,
Christ the Lord,
the new-born King."[140]

Charles Wesley put it this way:

"Veiled in flesh the Godhead see:
hail, the incarnate Deity,
pleased as Man with man to dwell,
Jesus, our Emmanuel."[141]

Today is Christmas Day. Jesus the Savior is born. The Word became flesh and dwelled among us.

---

[138] Hebrews 2:14-15, NKJV.
[139] From the hymn, "Angels We Have Heard on High," a French carol whose English version was provided by James Chadwick in 1862.
[140] Ibid.
[141] From the hymn, "Hark, the Herald Angels Sing," Charles Wesley, 1739.

30.

God Like Us

John 1:1-5, 9-14 RSV

¹ In the beginning was the Word, and the Word was with God, and the Word was God. ² He was in the beginning with God; ³ all things were made through him, and without him was not anything made that was made. ⁴ In him was life, and the life was the light of men. ⁵ The light shines in the darkness, and the darkness has not overcome it.

⁹ The true light that enlightens every man was coming into the world. ¹⁰ He was in the world, and the world was made through him, yet the world knew him not. ¹¹ He came to his own home, and his own people received him not. ¹² But to all who received him, who believed in his name, he gave power to become children of God; ¹³ who were born, not of blood nor of the will of the flesh nor of the will of man, but of God.

¹⁴ And the Word became flesh and dwelt among us, full of grace and truth; we have beheld his glory, glory as of the only Son from the Father.

☙❧

Last week, we heard from the Gospel of Matthew that a virgin would give birth to a child called "Emmanuel," which means "God with us."[142] God has always been with us, has always been an Emmanuel kind of God, though often we didn't know it or couldn't see it or wouldn't believe it.

And yet how fond we are of reading things like *Footprints in the Sand*.[143] But before, God had always been with us *as God*, occasionally appearing for some brief period of time in a physical form we would recognize, to accomplish a particular task or to make a specific point. Of course, nobody realized in these cases that they were dealing with God until later, when the prophecy came true or the chain of events God set in motion reached its intended conclusion. Then someone like Jacob would sit there stunned and say, *"the Lord is in this place, and I did not know it."*[144]

Today we read in the Gospel of John that *"the Word became flesh and dwelt among us."* This Word that John is talking about—this Word with a capital "W"—is not just a word. It's not what we think of when we think of words at all. John starts off his story of Jesus by introducing us to this Word, and defining it in a most unusual way. John says this Word was in the beginning; this Word was with God; in fact, this Word was God. This is no ordinary word.

The beginning John is talking about is the Creation of the world, the *very* beginning. According to John, this Word was already there when everything else came into existence. This Word was already there because this Word was a part of God Himself. This Word John is talking about is the sound of God saying *"Let there be light,"* and then light coming into being—light that never before existed.[145] This Word is the creative power of God.

John says this Word dwells among us. This is a reaffirmation of the truth we heard from Matthew: God is with us. The word for "dwell" is that old favorite they used for talking about the

---

[142] Matthew 1:18-23.
[143] *Footprints in the Sand* became widely known in the late 1970s. Its authorship is disputed.
[144] Genesis 28:16, RSV.
[145] Genesis 1:3.

tabernacle, that portable tent chapel Moses and the folks fell in behind as they marched around the wilderness all those years.[146] God was there with them, pitching His "tent" where they were, to show them that He was with them.

But John tells us more. He tells us something absolutely amazing, really. We're just so used to hearing it that we don't appreciate the significance of what we're being told. If the promise of Emmanuel is the promise of God *with* us, then the Word become flesh is the proof that "God is *like* us." "God with us" is the promise of His presence. "God like us" is the assurance of His understanding.

But God is not like us. In so many ways, this is so obviously true, I hesitate to even take the time to illustrate. God is eternal; we humans are mortal. The Psalmist says, "from everlasting to everlasting, thou art God," but "our years come to an end like a sigh."[147] God is all-knowing and all-powerful, and we are anything but.[148] God challenges Job: "Is it by your wisdom that the hawk soars...? Is it at your command that the eagle mounts up and makes his nest on high?"[149] And Job can only reply, "I am of small account; what shall I answer thee?"[150]

God is holy, while we are sinful.[151] Isaiah sums it up pretty well: "'...my thoughts are not your thoughts, neither are your ways my ways,' says the Lord. 'For as the heavens are higher than the earth, so are my ways higher than your ways and my thoughts than your thoughts.'"[152] It seems pretty clear that God is not like us.

---

[146] Exodus 25:8; 29:45.
[147] Psalm 90:2, 9, RSV.
[148] 1 Corinthians 1:25.
[149] Job 39:26-27, RSV.
[150] Job 40:4, RSV.
[151] 1 Samuel 2:2.
[152] Isaiah 55:8, RSV.

But we are created in the image of God.[153] And if it seems crazy to say that God is like us, maybe it's a little less crazy to try and make a case for saying that we are like God. God's plan for Creation ensures some similarity, some reflection of God in us. At our best, or perhaps in the best among us, there are hints of the godlikeness God had in mind when He created us. Generosity breaks out once in a while, especially at this time of year. Sometimes we consider things from a spiritual perspective. Occasionally, we get inspired by some idea or scene. We can at least imagine what God is like and what God thinks and feels.

But the truth is that we are not very much like God. Paul covered that pretty well in Chapter 3 of Romans.[154] Sin guarantees difference. We could not become like God again in any acceptable way, in the way that God intended and required when He created us in His image to begin with. Our sin dooms to failure every effort on our part to be God-like, just like the confusion of voices doomed the Babel tower project,[155] another famous humanity-to-God endeavor.

ఇ-ఇ

And then *the Word became flesh*—God became like us—so that we could understand enough about God's nature, God's plan and God's activity to cooperate with God in the process—His process—of making us like Him again. The Word became *flesh*, not a subjective vision or a subconscious dream or some disembodied voice in a burning bush. The essence of what God is became what we are. God lived and died, for all the divine uniqueness that is God, in the life and death of the individual human being Jesus, just like countless other very average and un-divine people before and since.

---

[153] Genesis 1:26-28.
[154] Romans 3:1-26.
[155] Genesis 11.

For Christmas Day

Why would we bother asking "What Would Jesus Do?" Because we think in this Word become flesh there's a chance that we could find and understand the answer.

What does it mean that God has become like us? We don't even know a lot of times what *we* are like. I changed the message on the church answering machine a few weeks ago and when I played it back, I thought I was listening to a staff member who left here almost a year ago (and is doing well, by the way). I had trouble recognizing my own voice. And that's not all people have trouble recognizing about themselves.

What does God being like us do for us? In my first tour as a Navy Chaplain, many years ago, I was assigned to a Marine infantry battalion. Also assigned to that battalion was the "ALO," the Air Liaison Officer. The ALO was a pilot who, up until he joined the battalion, had spent every bit of his career flying. The ALO was the one person among us who knew the "Air World." And he was the only person who could effectively bring the power of that world to bear on the needs of those on the ground. That Air Liaison Officer shared the life of the "grunts." He hiked in the heat and the rain, and he slept on the cold, hard ground. He ate his food out of those old green cans when he had to, just like everyone else. He became a grunt so that the grunts could benefit from the power from on high.

If you didn't think you were like God, well, now you can. You are like the Word Who became flesh. Not totally like, of course. There is that business of sin. But you are enough like this Word become flesh that you can get the essential picture of what God has in mind for you. You can do business with God about your sin, about His forgiving it and defeating it and taking its power away.

Does God understand what we feel when we suffer? Yes, He has felt that much and more. Does God understand what temptation feels like? Yes, it attacked Him as viciously as any one of us. Does God understand what we have to put up with from other people? Let me refer you to the Sadducees and the Pharisees and all those folks from His own hometown who told Him to "take a hike," and worse.

The only thing God doesn't understand from personal experience is sin.[156] But He certainly has an intimate knowledge of its consequences. He took on Himself the punishment for all our sins. That's what He came for; that's why God became like us.

Imitation is the sincerest form of flattery. So what does it say about the way God feels about us that He would lower Himself to become like us?[157]

Not that God came to flatter us. His imitation of our humanity in Jesus was for something far better than flattery. It was for our salvation, pure and simple—the right to become the children of God.

---

[156] Hebrews 4:14-15.
[157] Philippians 2:5-8.

The Sunday after Christmas

Born that Men No More May Die

Hebrews 2:10-18 ESV

¹⁰ *For it was fitting that he, for whom and by whom all things exist, in bringing many sons to glory, should make the founder of their salvation perfect through suffering.* ¹¹ *For he who sanctifies and those who are sanctified all have one source. That is why he is not ashamed to call them brothers,* ¹² *saying,*

> *"I will tell of your name to my brothers;*
> *in the midst of the congregation*
> *I will sing your praise."*

¹³ *And again,*

> *"I will put my trust in him."*

And again,

> *"Behold, I and the children God has given me."*

¹⁴ *Since therefore the children share in flesh and blood, he himself likewise partook of the same things, that through death he might destroy the one who has the power of death, that is, the devil,* ¹⁵ *and deliver all those who through fear of death were subject to lifelong slavery.* ¹⁶ *For surely it is not angels that he helps, but he helps the offspring of Abraham.* ¹⁷ *Therefore he had to be made like his brothers in every respect, so that he might become a merciful and faithful high priest in the service of God, to make propitiation for the sins of the people.* ¹⁸ *For because he himself has suffered when tempted, he is able to help those who are being tempted.*

31.

Born that Men No More May Die

Hebrews 2:10-18 ESV

You would think they would give you just a little time to enjoy the beauty and magic of Christmas[158]—just a little time to marvel at the Messiah in the manger and promote a little *"peace on earth, good will toward men."*[159] But no; it's kind of like a windshield tour of the Grant Canyon: "Take a look—time to go."

Poor Joseph barely gets the last wise man back on his camel[160] before that angel shows up in a dream again and tells him to pack up his new family and run away to Egypt. And can't you just hear Joseph thinking: "Do you have any idea what the traffic is going to be like the day after Christmas?!"

Yesterday, it was all "Joy to the World, the Lord is Come"[161] and "Sing We Now of Christmas."[162] A day later, as we watch Mary and Joseph hightailing it out of town with the Baby,[163] we're wondering…

---

[158] This sermon was preached on Sunday, December 26th.
[159] Luke 2:14, KJV.
[160] Matthew 2:12-13.
[161] "Joy to the World," Isaac Watts (from Psalm 98), 1719.
[162] "Sing We Now of Christmas" is from a French carol of the 15th Century. The English translator is unknown.
[163] Matthew 2:14.

"why Jesus the Savior did come for to die."[164]

And Herod's soldiers are certainly not humming "O come, let us adore Him" as they hurry down to Bethlehem, trying to catch up with this newborn King[165] and "nip *Him* in the bud."[166]

Jesus the Savior is born, but there really isn't much time for quiet contemplation about the meaning of it all. Jesus is born, and immediately, the business for which He has been born begins.

Jesus has been born to overthrow a terribly dangerous tyrant— a tyrant who will not go down without a fight. This tyrant—also known as the prince of darkness, the ruler of this world, or simply, the devil—will call on every principality and power under his control to stop this Baby from fulfilling the purpose for which God has caused Him to be born into the human race.

It's a fascinating thing: powerful forces, human and otherwise, want Jesus dead—for their purposes—and, at the same time, God Himself has sent Jesus to die, though for a very different purpose. The devil and all who serve him want Jesus dead from the minute He's born—sooner, if possible. But Jesus, Who has been born to die, is not ready—not qualified—as a Baby, to accomplish what God wants—and we need—the death of Jesus to accomplish.

And so God will protect Jesus until Jesus is able to fulfill His divinely-appointed human destiny. God will protect Jesus until Jesus is able to die the death God always intended for Jesus to die—the death for which Jesus has been born.

"But couldn't they give us just a little time to savor the splendor of Christmas?"

Savor all you want, but the sooner God gets down to business and gets Jesus ready to be our Savior, the better it will be for all of us who spend our lives pressed down like slaves under the thumb of the devil. You see, God had a purpose in having the second Person of the Godhead, the equally eternal and absolutely infinite

---

[164] From the hymn, "I Wonder as I Wander," John Jacob Niles, 1933.
[165] Matthew 2:16-17.
[166] A line used frequently by the Barney Fife character on *The Andy Griffith Show*.

Son, lay aside His divine glory and become man.[167] God had a purpose in the pre-existent Word's allowing Himself to be formed as a human embryo in the womb of a woman who was, like every other person in existence, totally dependent upon His divine graciousness for her very life and breath.

God's purpose was nothing less than destroying the devil and the devil's power to hold every human being in permanent slavery to our fear of death.

Great purpose, but it requires a plan—a plan that will work—a plan that will preserve God's righteousness while it provides for His loving mercy to perform the miracle He wants to perform, with the power to "do the devil in," despite the devil's every effort to derail the plan.

And God had such a plan. It required a Man. It required a Man Who, because He was a Man, would fear death, and yet a Man Who could overcome that fear—and die, willingly. It required a Man Who would be like everyone in some basic human way—and yet would not, Himself, deserve to die because of His own personal sin. God's plan required a Man, a human Being, because a God Who is the Lord of life *and* death—and so cannot die—cannot fear death, either.

The devil, that old deceiver, wants you to believe that *he* controls death. But it isn't so:

> *"The Lord giveth and the Lord taketh away—*
> *blessed be the name of the Lord."* [168]

God controls death; the devil merely controls and manipulates the *fear* of death in us, which is bad enough, because our primal fear of death as human beings leaves us vulnerable to all sorts of the devil's temptations. Our fear of death enables the devil to enslave us all our lives—until and unless we are set free by One Who knows that fear, but is not enslaved by it. This One Who can

---

[167] Philippians 2:5-8.
[168] Job 1:21, KJV.

and will die in our place must be enough like us to be able to die in our place. He must share fully in our human condition.

And yet, He can't be like us in sinfulness, one basic aspect of humanity, because then He will have to die for His own sins, which doesn't do any of the rest of us any good.[169] That's what we're going to have to do ourselves anyway—die for our sins[170]—unless something happens to change everything.

God solved that problem. The Savior could not be a sinner and still be a Savior, but He could be like everyone else in another way—by being a Person Who suffers.

Who of us does not suffer? You may not see your neighbor's suffering, but you certainly know your own. Trust me on this one: everybody suffers. Other people may not suffer enough to satisfy you, but I can assure you, they will be perfectly satisfied that their suffering has been sufficient.

And funny that the word "perfect" should pop up in a discussion of suffering, because the writer of Hebrews says that *"God perfected Jesus as the Author of our salvation **through suffering**."* It's funny, because you would think Jesus as the Son of God would have been *born* perfect. Remember: "*Holy* Infant so tender and mild."[171] And, of course, He *was* born perfect, in all moral and spiritual senses, as perfect as the God He is.

But Jesus at birth was not yet qualified in all ways to be the Author of our salvation and the Pioneer of our faith. At birth, Jesus was not yet perfect for the task God sent Him to perform.

God took perfect divinity and combined it with humanity in a Person Who had then to be perfected through suffering in order to be the perfect and acceptable Sacrifice to atone for humanity and break the back of sin.

---

[169] 2 Corinthians 5:21.
[170] Genesis 2:15-17; Romans 5:12, 18.
[171] From the hymn, "Silent Night," Franz Gruber and Joseph Mohr, 1818. The English translation was provided by John Freeman Young in 1859.

The Sunday After Christmas

As Luke said in the familiar Christmas story, *"the time came for the Baby to be born."*[172] And what the writer of Hebrews is saying, with somewhat more complexity, is, "the time came when the One born to be our Savior—the One 'born that men no more may die'[173]—was ready and qualified to die for us." When all was right—when all was ready—God executed the plan for which Jesus had been conceived and born—and God's purpose in coming to us in human form was achieved.

❧

And what was the devil doing all this time?

Well, he wasn't going to after-Christmas sales—(or maybe he was, if the level of temptation is any indication). He was certainly doing everything he could to spoil God's plan and thwart God's purpose and retain his own chokehold on humanity. When the devil's minions were not trying to figure out a way to kill Jesus, they were setting up roadblocks and booby traps to trip Jesus up and halt His progress to the place in time and space and God's will where He would fulfill the promise of His birth. When the devil could not control Jesus with the fear of death, the devil turned those he could control loose on Jesus to take His life and silence His message.

But you shouldn't play the "death card" with the Lord of life and death. The devil did his worst at the Cross to make the birth in Bethlehem a bust. But he only gave God the final opening God had foreseen and planned for to destroy the devil's power over us. By the power of the rebirth of Jesus in the Resurrection, God fulfilled the purpose for the birth of Jesus in the stable years before.

> "What Child is this
> who, laid to rest,
> on Mary's lap is sleeping?"[174]

---

[172] Luke 2:6.
[173] From the hymn, "Hark, the Herald Angels Sing," Charles Wesley, 1739.
[174] From the hymn, "What Child is This?" William Chatterton Dix, 1865.

Well…as the song says,
> "This, this, is Christ the King,
> Whom shepherds guard and angels sing."[175]

But know something else about what Child this is:
> "Nails, spear shall pierce Him through,
> the Cross be borne for me, for you."[176]

God sent Jesus to be born into our world and to live our life so that God Himself would be like us in every respect and, as our loving Brother, be able to sacrifice Himself for us and save us from the sin the devil had used to enslave us.

❧

The devil has been defeated—his power destroyed. But he's hoping you don't know that.

The devil is hoping he can continue to bluff you into keeping the shackles of fear firmly in place, even though the locks have been opened and the key thrown away.

Bluffing us became a whole lot harder after the birth of the Baby in Bethlehem, because the Baby didn't stay in the manger, or in the swaddling clothes, or in Bethlehem, for that matter.

He didn't stay in infancy or childhood or adolescence any longer than He had to, to learn what His Heavenly Father wanted Him to learn. And the Baby born at Christmas didn't even stay among us as a Man any longer than it took for God to perfect Him, through His suffering, to be our acceptable Sacrifice and the Author of our salvation.

So linger a little longer with the Babe in the manger, and visit as you like with the familiar folks of Christmas. But know that what happened in Bethlehem was not the end of a process; it was only the human beginning of an age-old plan.

If you are inspired by the birth of the Christmas Child, then believe in the Man the Child becomes and follow Him where He

---
[175] Ibid.
[176] Ibid.

leads you. There's nothing to hold you back. There's nothing to fear. He made sure of that.

Follow Jesus, the perfect Pioneer of your salvation, and He'll bring you to the glory God always intended for you.

32.

What Did You Get for Christmas?

Galatians 4:4-7 NRSV

⁴ But when the fullness of time had come, God sent his Son, born of a woman, born under the law, ⁵ in order to redeem those who were under the law, so that we might receive adoption as children. ⁶ And because you are children, God has sent the Spirit of his Son into our hearts, crying, "Abba! Father!" ⁷ So you are no longer a slave but a child, and if a child then also an heir, through God.

☙❧

Well, here we are—the Sunday after Christmas. I don't know the liturgical calendar well enough to know if today has a special title or designation. We could just call it "Exhaustion Sunday."

If you didn't wear yourself out cooking or baking, you probably outdid yourself eating the culinary contributions of others. Wonderful family gatherings (as wonderful as they are) can generate an awful lot of wear and tear on the body and the emotions, whether you're hosting, or traveling, or waiting for the weather to let you travel to where you can be hosted.

And then there's the business of presents. If you're going to give presents, you've got to get the presents you're going to give.

At least, that's what women tell me. They tell me it's called "shopping."

However all the presents get under the trees and in the stockings, by the time we get them out of the stockings and away from the trees and unwrapped, most of us are exhausted. We are exhausted from the preparation for Christmas—and the anticipation of it. Even children, who don't do a lot of preparing for Christmas, are pretty exhausted by now from all their anticipation of it—even though they thought it would never get here.

But it did. Christmas has come, and this is the Sunday after. And now, a bit worn out by all the preparation and anticipation—and celebration—we have time to review and evaluate. We have time to consider the impact—and tally up the results.

The kids are already at it. Get two together and one of them will invariably ask the other, "What did you get?" When they go back to school next week, they will put the presidential pollsters to shame as they gather the collective data about who got what for Christmas.

But the kids aren't the only ones with the time to review and evaluate. Christmas has come—and we who have a few more Christmases under our belts will do our own inventories, in more subtle ways. We will tally up our Christmas, and our categories will be more sophisticated than those of our children and grandchildren.

You may have reached the stage in life where toys take a back seat to less tangible and more personal things, like the quality of your time with those you love. You may not be able to match the excitement of a four-year-old bounding out of bed on Christmas morning, but your heart can be filled with a joy that the little ones simply cannot imagine.

But let's take it deeper.

The Sunday After Christmas

Christmas has come—which means Christ has come. And this is a good Sunday to consider the impact of His coming, and tally up the results, not of what we have given each other, but of what God has given us.

What presents did God give you, when all the preparations He had made across time were completed, and the centuries of human anticipation was fulfilled? What did you get for Christmas—from God?

Paul said, *"When the fullness of time had come, God sent his Son, born of woman, born under law."* He's talking about Christmas.

Here's what God gave you for Christmas. God sent His Son. You can send presents anywhere in the country. Give UPS or FED-EX a street address and they'll delivery your present right to someone's front door. On the other hand, God sent His Son to the womb of a woman—and to your heart and life—and He didn't need your zip code to do it.

We like to say: the greatest gift you can give is the gift of yourself. Here's your proof, infinitely magnified. The One Who was from-all-eternity-God, became as human as you can get, in order to give Himself to and for you.

But this was not one of those "What do I do with *this*?" kind of gifts. God's Christmas gift to you of His Son is a present with a purpose: *"God sent his Son...to redeem those who were under law."*

We better unwrap that a little bit because the world doesn't talk that way anymore. That's not to say it isn't true, it just means that we've denied and ignored the fact that we're "under law" so well for so long that most people are convinced now that we really aren't under it anymore.

And yet, there *is* a law that the world and all of us in it are under. This law is simply "the way reality works." It is the way God Himself set things up for the world He created, so that it and we would work together effectively on this planet.

We cannot eliminate, change or avoid this law of things. It determines the consequences of our actions as individuals and societies. To violate this divine law is to damage the processes God designed for productive and satisfying life on earth. It is, at the same time, to anger the Creator of this world Who has made us aware of this law's existence.

Every human being is subject to this law, and every human being (save One) has violated it. Every human being has suffered the consequences of our transgression against this law. We cannot keep this law and we cannot make it up to God for breaking it.

And so God sends His Son Who can both keep the law, and make it up to God, for us. In Jesus, for Christmas, God has given us redemption—at no small expense to Himself. He has paid, not just our bail, but the whole fine—in full.

What did you get for Christmas? The gift of God's Son—and the gift of redemption from your penalty under the law.

Now get this picture: You're locked up for something you did—guilty as sin and they got you dead to rights. Some nice guy comes along and gets you out and somehow also gets all the charges dropped.

Then instead of sending you on your way with a stern warning to do better next time and a little pocket change to get you by for a while, he takes you to his house to meet his dad, who, it turns out, was the one who sent the nice guy to spring you in the first place.

So you're pinching yourself and wondering how you got so lucky all of a sudden, and the guy's dad says, "Welcome home, son."

But he's not talking to the guy who paid for your freedom; he's talking to you: "Welcome home, daughter." "You don't have to go back to where you came from," the father is saying. "You don't have to live the life you've been living."

"My purpose in sending my son to free you was to adopt you as my own child. I'm giving you a new identity and a new future

The Sunday After Christmas

for Christmas. You will be my child—a member of my family—and you will share equally in all I have to give my children."[177]

☙❧

What did you get for Christmas? The gift of God's Son, Jesus. Redemption from bondage to and punishment under the law. Adoption as a child of God. Already it sounds like a MOLAB Christmas. That's MOLAB, spelled M-O-L-A-B, as in "made-out-like-a-bandit."

But there's more.

Paul says, *"Because you are God's children, God has sent the Spirit of his Son into your hearts."* (I mentioned that pinpoint shipping ability of God before.)

You got the gift of God's Son to redeem you from the terrible fix you were in. Then, after adopting you as His own child, God sends you the gift of the Holy Spirit like one of these "confirmation card" you get to assure you that you really are going to get the present promised to you. But God doesn't send the Spirit to your post office box or your front porch; the Spirit goes special delivery, straight into your heart.[178]

And the Holy Spirit isn't just sitting there watching the bowl games! He is creating fast, reliable and permanent connectivity between you and the Heavenly Father Who has adopted you as His very own. You don't have to walk around wondering, "Can He hear me now?" You have the Holy Spirit in your heart going, "Abba, Father!" all the time. And your "Abba"—your Father in heaven—is listening all the time—to you and the Holy Spirit in you—because you are His child—His beloved child.

What did you get for Christmas?

---

[177] John 1:12-13.
[178] John 14:15-17; Romans 5:3-5.

You got Jesus, God's Son, sent to you. You got redemption from the burden and penalty of the moral and spiritual law of the Creation that *none* of us can keep. You got adopted as a child of God with all the benefits, privileges and promises due to a child of God. You got the gift of the Spirit of Christ in your heart to confirm all the rest of it.

You made out like a—

O wait, there is a little catch.

To get these Christmas presents, you have to accept them. You have to pull them out of the package they came in. Full stockings after Christmas are just silly. Unopened presents under the tree on Exhaustion Sunday don't make sense. Christmas has come.

Christmas has come. Christ has come—and He has brought you some wonderful gifts. What did you get for Christmas? What did you get from Christ?

The Sunday After Christmas

Luke 2:41-52 ESV

⁴¹ Now [Jesus'] parents went to Jerusalem every year at the Feast of the Passover. ⁴² And when he was twelve years old, they went up according to custom. ⁴³ And when the feast was ended, as they were returning, the boy Jesus stayed behind in Jerusalem. His parents did not know it, ⁴⁴ but supposing him to be in the group they went a day's journey, but then they began to search for him among their relatives and acquaintances, ⁴⁵ and when they did not find him, they returned to Jerusalem, searching for him. ⁴⁶ After three days they found him in the temple, sitting among the teachers, listening to them and asking them questions. ⁴⁷ And all who heard him were amazed at his understanding and his answers. ⁴⁸ And when his parents saw him, they were astonished. And his mother said to him, "Son, why have you treated us so? Behold, your father and I have been searching for you in great distress." ⁴⁹ And he said to them, "Why were you looking for me? Did you not know that I must be in my Father's house?" ⁵⁰ And they did not understand the saying that he spoke to them. ⁵¹ And he went down with them and came to Nazareth and was submissive to them. And his mother treasured up all these things in her heart.

⁵² And Jesus increased in wisdom and in stature and in favor with God and man.

33.

What's Got into That Boy?

Luke 2:41-52 ESV

Well, the holidays are over. Everybody is heading home. It was a wonderful celebration and everybody enjoyed it. But to be honest, fatigue is the order of the day, and most people, as much as they enjoyed the festivities, are ready to get back to normal.

Mary and Joseph are among them. They made their annual pilgrimage to Jerusalem for Passover, the biggest holiday of the year. (Christmas hasn't caught on yet; and Easter hasn't even happened.) When they went to Bethlehem the year that Jesus was born, they went alone. But this year—12 years later—just about everybody from Nazareth went down to Jerusalem together for the big celebration—or "up to Jerusalem," as the Jews like to say.

They went on the "friends and family" plan, which is cheaper for everybody, and like in the '50s, everybody looks after everybody else's kids and nothing bad ever happens. But whoever took the head count on the way back didn't quite get it right. At the end of the first day on the road, there's one missing: Jesus.

The second day on the road is more like the trip to Bethlehem: Mary and Joseph are alone again, on their way back, looking for Jesus. Day three, they find Him, but their attitude is a bit different from that of the shepherds who found Jesus as a baby in the manger in Bethlehem.[179]

True, the shepherds were amazed when they found what the angels had told them—and Mary and Joseph are amazed to find their 12-year-old Son sitting in a graduate seminar on theology at the Temple. The shepherds gave glory to God for the good news they had heard and seen, but what the earthly parents of the 12-year-old Son of God in their custody give Him is not exactly "glory"—it's more like a piece of their minds for scaring them so, despite what they are seeing and hearing as they find Him.

And Jesus—even at 12 years of age—has something to say to them that will surprise them and perplex them. He will tell them something they really need to know—something they don't know, apparently, even after all the years they've spent with Him.

"Why didn't you know where to find Me?" says Jesus. "I must be in My Father's house. I must be about my Father's business."

Just when you think you know where Jesus is—just when you think you know what He's going to do—just when you take for granted that He is going to go wherever you're going—you look around and He's not where you expect Him to be—He's not doing what you want Him to be doing.

"Wasn't the holiday great? Don't you just love everything about it—the joy and celebration?"

"Yes, it was wonderful and I wouldn't have missed any of it. But now, let's pack it all up and get back to normal. Come on, Jesus. Let's go home. Jesus! Jesus, where are You?"

If Jesus isn't with you as you head back to the old routine, you will need to go find Him. Retrace your steps to the place where you were last aware that He was with you.

---

[179] Luke 2:16-20.

The Sunday After Christmas

The prophet Isaiah recommended: *"Seek...the LORD while he may be found."*[180]

We might just as well say, "Seek the Lord *where* He may be found." Where is Jesus going to be when you realize you've lost touch with Him?

In His Father's house; involved in His Father's business. You see, that's where Jesus *must* be. As the grown-up Jesus will tell Pilate, *"...for this purpose I was born and for this purpose I have come into the world."*[181] And this much—where He must be and what He must be about—Jesus understood, even at 12.

And here's the good news: The grown-up Jesus will tell those listening to His Sermon on the Mount: *"Seek and you will find,"*[182] which is not unlike the promise recorded in the Book of the prophet Jeremiah: *"You will seek me and find me when you seek me with all your heart."*[183]

But, of course, Mary and Joseph and even Jesus couldn't spend the rest of their lives in the Temple. You can't spend all your life here in God's house (we lock the place up and turn on the security alarms).

Jesus did go back home with Mary and Joseph—*after* He had made His point. And He will go home with you—when you understand that whether He is in the Temple in Jerusalem or His own home in Nazareth or your home—your life—here, He will still be—*must* be—about His Father's business.

Now that's something to put in your heart and ponder—as Mary did—as they went home—with Jesus.

---

[180] Isaiah 55:6, KJV.
[181] John 18:37, ESV.
[182] Matthew 7:7, ESV.
[183] Jeremiah 29:13, ESV.

34.

Looking for Jesus—Finding the Christ

Luke 2:41-52 ESV (p. 221)

Have you ever noticed how time hurries by during the holidays? For instance, on Friday, Jesus was a newborn Baby. Today,[184] He's a twelve-year-old Boy.

His parents must have thought, as many of us do watching kids grow up, "Where did the time go?" After their journey to Jerusalem for the Passover holiday, Mary and Joseph were also wondering, "Where did *He* go?"

It just goes to show that even the best parents—the best parents of all time—can have some bad moments. The man and woman closer to Jesus than anyone else in all the world—the people who know Him better than anybody—all of a sudden realize they've lost sight of Him.

Rarely has He been out of their sight since the holy night He was born to them. But if He isn't right there with them now, they're confident He's nearby, in the midst of their broader family or community who care for Him just as much as they do.

---

[184] This sermon was preached on Sunday, December 27th.

You go with Jesus to and through a wonderful religious ritual. You're on your way back home—back to the normal routine. You're still feeling the joy of what you've just experienced.

How could Jesus not be with you?

And yet, there you are one day—the muster sheets are complete, and Jesus simply isn't anywhere you expect Him to be. That Mary and Joseph can't find Him *one time* is surprising enough that it's worth mentioning in the Bible. But if you and I are honest, we lose track of Jesus a lot more often than that.

After a big holiday—or any old day—you can get so distracted or disgruntled or depressed that your point of view just doesn't have room for Jesus. All you can see is yourself and your concerns—or other people and theirs—looming larger than life—and certainly larger than they or you ever deserve to be—or should be allowed to be—if you're not to lose sight of Jesus.

Or maybe there's no negligence involved at all. Maybe for no reason you can discern, Jesus just isn't "there." He said that He would be *"with you always."*[185] So where is He?

Mary and Joseph know Jesus isn't where they thought He would be—where they want Him to be—which is with them—so they do the most logical thing: they go looking for Him. And in doing so, they have set all of us who lose track of Jesus a good example: If you can't find Jesus, go looking for Him. Don't just assume He'll turn up, sooner or later. That's too big a risk.

Mary and Joseph stop what they're doing. They turn around from where they've been going. They leave the people they've been hanging out with. And they go looking for Jesus.

Now let's be honest, the method Mary and Joseph use is more like looking for a needle in a haystack. They clearly don't know how to conduct a systematic search in an efficient and effective manner. They canvas the vast capital city of Jerusalem for days, hoping to happen upon one particular 12-year-old Boy. They don't

---

[185] Matthew 28:20, ESV.

have a clue what they're doing. But, in time, God guides them to Jesus anyway.

It's amazing how long it takes Mary and Joseph to think to look for Jesus in the Temple—the house of God. Where else are they looking—and why? They've been told by angels Who He is. They know what He's here for. "Why didn't you know where to find Me?" says Jesus. *"I must be in my Father's house. I must be about my Father's business."*

☙❧

We'll get back to that—but notice that what they learn when they do find Jesus can teach you a lot about how to go looking for Jesus more effectively when you realize that's what you need to be doing. If you're looking for Jesus, the house of God is a pretty good place to start your search. *"I must be in my Father's house."*

The Temple in Jerusalem is long gone, of course. It was already gone—destroyed—even before Luke wrote his gospel.

This church will do well enough now. It, too, is the Father's House, though on a significantly simpler scale. Our heavenly Father has chosen to make His presence felt here—to cause His Holy Spirit to hover about us and His holy Word to be hidden within us. This is a good place—though not at all the only place—to look for Jesus successfully.

The key, of course, is to actually look. There were apparently quite a few people who went to the Jerusalem Temple who weren't really looking for Jesus—when He was a Baby—or a Boy—or a Man in His full maturity.

Old Simeon and Anna were looking for Him, of course[186]—as were Mary and Joseph, as we've read. Pilgrims were enthusiastically looking for Him when He showed up there for His last Passover—though the money-changers and the chief priests, just as surely, were not.[187]

---

[186] Luke 2:22-40.
[187] Luke 19:45-48.

Many people today—it seems—have no interest in looking for Jesus, and that's a shame—and worse. Everybody who realizes that Jesus is not "there" should be looking for Jesus. You can't make them look if they don't want to, but you could encourage them to want to—at least a little.

And let me let you in on a little secret: a lot of people may tell you they're not looking for Jesus, but an awful lot of people are looking for *something* today—desperately looking. And though the one thing they're sure of is that Jesus is not What or Who they're looking for—they're actually wrong. Most people who are looking for things like "Mr. Right," or "love in all the wrong places," or "answers," won't find what they're looking for without finding Jesus first.

Neither you nor anyone else will be "right" until you find Jesus and let Him make you "right." Every place you look for love will be the wrong place unless you find Jesus there, too.

And the only answers worth finding in this life are the ones you find when you find Him.

And why is that?

Because when you go looking for Jesus, Who you find is Christ.

Mary and Joseph go back to Jerusalem to look for their 12-year-old Son. Three days later, they discover a Boy in the Temple Who bears a striking resemblance to *their* Boy, yet the Boy they find in the Temple is astonishing the greatest theologians of the day—and them. The tenured teachers are teaching, but this Boy's questions indicate that He is way ahead of them.

They are scholars, well-versed in the Law; He is the Savior, a Son sent from the God Who gave them the Law.

Mary points to Joseph beside her and tells Jesus, "Your father and I were distressed when You weren't where we thought You would be." And Jesus points heavenward and replies, "My Father knows where I am and that I am exactly where He wants Me to be."

They've been looking for their Son, Jesus. They find *God's* Son—the Christ.

☙❧

What are you looking for when you come to this place? What are you looking for when you lift your heart in worship or bow your head in prayer? What are you looking for when you read what Jesus said and did in the Bible, or copy Him, as best you can, in your own words and deeds?

By all means, look for Jesus when you feel like you've lost Him. And don't be surprised if Jesus doesn't "stay where you put Him." Just realize that when you look for Jesus, God intends that you will find His Christ—not just a nice Boy—or Man—Who will keep you company and calms your fears as you travel through "this world of woe."[188]

You will find the Christ Who has amazing answers that will overwhelm your most curious questions. You will find the Christ Who will take your mind and heart and soul far beyond man's understanding of religious things to revelations of holy things only heaven can conceive. God will give you a Christ Who, though first a Baby, and then a Boy—became a Man Whose sacrificial death destroyed the hold of sin over your life and every life, now and forever.

Mary says to Jesus, *"Son, why have you treated us so?"*

Jesus answers her, *"Why were you looking for me."*

It's an odd exchange for a 12-year-old boy to have with his mother, under the (human) circumstances. It just goes to show that even those who think they know Jesus best still have a lot to learn about Him.

And for His part, Jesus doesn't understand why they, of all people, didn't come to God's house first to find Him. The best and

---

[188] From the tradition folk/gospel song, "Wayfarin' Stranger," circa early 1800s.

most effective way to look for Jesus is to understand that Who He is will determine where He will be.

But there's more to it than that. You see, you may think that you are the one looking for Jesus when you sense the emptiness only He can fill. But the truth is that long before you ever thought of looking for Jesus—and many times when you don't think of looking for Him now—Jesus is looking for you. That's what God sent Him to do—*"to seek and to save that which was lost"*[189]—as the King James puts it.

Jesus doesn't get lost. He is always where God wants Him to be—always being the Christ God sent Him into this life to be. And the Christ Who is Jesus is always looking for you—to accomplish your salvation—your redemption and transformation and reconciliation with God. And in the course of this lifelong searching of Jesus Christ for you, He will cause you to feel the joy and wonder of being found by the God Who refuses to give up in His search for you, wherever you go—whatever you've done.

Mary and Joseph go looking for their Jesus and they find so very much more—so much more that they will have to think for quite a while about the meaning of those three days when they thought they had lost Him—which is okay, because they are going to have an eternity to do so, because they have let their Christ find them.

The Boy Jesus goes home with His human parents, which suggests a happy ending to this biblical story: they have found each other.

And years later, when the disciples of a very grown-up Jesus—including Mary, His mother—come to the end of another Passover in Jerusalem and think—for an agonizing three days—that they have lost Jesus for good, perhaps the memory of His boyhood assurance to her that He has to be about His Father's business

---

[189] Luke 19:10, KJV.

encourages her to keep looking for her Jesus, until she finds her Christ—or He finds her—again and forever.

Epiphany

Isaiah 52:7-10 ESV

⁷ How beautiful upon the mountains
  are the feet of him
    who brings good news,
    who publishes peace,
    who brings good news of happiness,
    who publishes salvation,
    who says to Zion, "Your God reigns."
⁸ The voice of your watchmen—
  they lift up their voice;
  together they sing for joy;
    for eye to eye they see
    the return of the LORD to Zion.
⁹ Break forth together into singing,
  you waste places of Jerusalem,
    for the LORD has comforted his people;
    he has redeemed Jerusalem.
¹⁰ The LORD has bared his holy arm
  before the eyes of all the nations,
  and all the ends of the earth shall see
    the salvation of our God.

Going a Different Way

Matthew 2:1-12 ESV

¹ Now after Jesus was born in Bethlehem of Judea in the days of Herod the king, behold, wise men from the east came to Jerusalem, ² saying, "Where is he who has been born king of the Jews? For we saw his star when it rose and have come to worship him." ³ When Herod the king heard this, he was troubled, and all Jerusalem with him; ⁴ and assembling all the chief priests and scribes of the people, he inquired of them where the Christ was to be born. ⁵ They told him, "In Bethlehem of Judea, for so it is written by the prophet:

> ⁶ 'And you, O Bethlehem, in the land of Judah,
> are by no means least among the rulers of Judah;
> for from you shall come a ruler
> who will shepherd my people Israel.'"

⁷ Then Herod summoned the wise men secretly and ascertained from them what time the star had appeared. ⁸ And he sent them to Bethlehem, saying, "Go and search diligently for the child, and when you have found him, bring me word, that I too may come and worship him." ⁹ After listening to the king, they went on their way. And behold, the star that they had seen when it rose went before them until it came to rest over the place where the child was. ¹⁰ When they saw the star, they rejoiced exceedingly with great joy. ¹¹ And going into the house, they saw the child with Mary his mother, and they fell down and worshiped him. Then, opening their treasures, they offered him gifts, gold and frankincense and myrrh. ¹² And being warned in a dream not to return to Herod, they departed to their own country by another way.

35.

Going a Different Way

Isaiah 52:7-10; Matthew 2:1-3, 7-12 ESV

Now that we all have our GPS devices, in our cars or on our phones, we can find our way anywhere. Or so you would think.

All you have to do is input your desired destination into your miracle machine and it will determine the way you are to go. You can pick a location—a specific address—hopefully, one that actually exists—hopefully, the correct one—and it will show you how to get there. You can pick the *kind* of place to which you want to go—a store, a restaurant, a park or playground—and your GPS will find the nearest one. You can choose *how* you want to go—whether the shortest route or the quickest—staying on major highways or avoiding them—and it won't be long before the right route is laid out for you. Now that we all have GPS, we should always get where we want to go.

So how do you get to happiness—or peace—or reconciliation—or contentment—or courage? How do you find your way to hope—or respect—or integrity—or love—or any of the states we all want to get to, but no GPS will take you?

Just about everybody was on the road these past few days, going near or far, headed some place that was not nearly as important as the purpose for which each journey was undertaken.

And no matter how many times that pleasant little voice said, "You have arrived at your destination," many people knew, deep in their hearts, they still were not where they wanted to be.

When the Bible tells the story of the birth of Jesus—the long-awaited coming of God from heaven to earth—a lot of other individuals are also set in motion. Mary goes to see her relative, Elizabeth.[190] Mary and Joseph go from Nazareth to Bethlehem[191]—and later, from Bethlehem to Egypt[192]—and later still, from Egypt back to Nazareth.[193] Angels go from heaven to points all over Palestine. Shepherds go from grazing fields to a glowing stable and then all over town telling what they saw.[194] And fascinating foreigners find a star that starts them on a quest to find the One Who will change their world forever.[195]

Their astrology will lead these last to Jerusalem. The scripture of the Jews will lead them to Bethlehem and the Baby they seek.[196] And a dream will provide the divine direction that will lead them home—a different way.[197]

☙❧

What can we learn from these learned individuals—these wise men—from the East?

These were men who carefully observed the wonders of their world and found in what they saw the first few steps in a fateful journey of faith. They saw a star rising—a natural phenomenon.

---

[190] Luke 1:39-40.
[191] Luke 2:4-5.
[192] Matthew 2:14-15.
[193] Matthew 2:21-23.
[194] Luke 2:8-20.
[195] Matthew 2:1-2, 9-11.
[196] Micah 5:2-5.
[197] Matthew 2:12.

Epiphany

They saw something happen and assumed it had some significance in their world and in their lives. They were wise to think so, even though natural occurrences never tell you all you need to know about the way you need to go.

It is a wise person who pays attention to the signs of the times—who assumes that there is meaning in all that takes place. The Creator of all things created all things to conform to, and serve, a particular purpose in a perfect plan. There is, in all created things, evidence still of the Creator, and some faint echo of His original purpose, even after Creation's catastrophic fall.

For the wise men of old, whose business was to study the heavens, the rising of a special star was just such an echo, an omen, a suggestion that something divine was in the offing. And they charted a course, according to the light they had been given, inadequate as it was, to lead them to their ultimate destination.

They did not wait where they were until they understood everything about where they were to go. They saw enough in the world they knew to do something different than they had been doing. God sent them a sign in the natural world around them, and from that moment, they began going a different way to find out more.

Today, or tomorrow, or next week or next year, something will happen in the life of every person that will be God's sign, signaling that person to go a different way. Many will think nothing of it—ignore it as just an accident of fate—a coincidence, signifying nothing significant or sacred. They will go on exactly as before.

But some will wonder: *why* did this happen; and *what* does it mean; and *what* should I do about it? And some of those will start going a different way—and take the first faltering but essential steps in a journey that will bring them face to face with God—just as God intends.

The wise men, having seen a star that suggested to them they needed to make a change, went to Jerusalem, the holy city. The star did not lead them there.[198] They just knew they needed to consult the religious experts to get more guidance about the way they should go.

"General revelation"—God communicating His character and will in nature and the otherwise routine events of life—motivated them to get started doing what God wanted them to do. But it would take "special revelation"—the word of God recorded in sacred scripture—to show them where they would find the goal of their spiritual quest. It was the Bible that led them to Bethlehem—and to Jesus.

All sorts of people may experience an occasional impulse toward religion and moral living. If all people are created in the image of God—as the Bible reveals[199]—then there must be a spiritual dimension in every one of us—a capacity to interact with God.

Unfortunately, our religious impulses—corrupted as they are by our human sinfulness—are insufficient, in power or purity, to satisfy God. The way we go about gratifying our inadequate religious inclinations on our own won't work with God.

On the other hand, fortunately, God's Word leads us to the place where our unworthy efforts and inclinations can be corrected and completed by God's Incarnation in Jesus, so that we are made acceptable—to Him—by Him. The wise men didn't find God's Messiah in "the East"—the familiar surroundings of their homes and work, where wisdom was valued above all else. They did not

---

[198] In *The Birth of the Messiah*, (Doubleday & Co., Inc, Garden City, New York, 1977), respected New Testament scholar Raymond E. Brown discusses the historical background of the star of the wise men in detail (pp. 170-174). He suggests that the wise men may have gone to Jerusalem because they understood the location in the sky or the composition of the star, comet or conjunction of planets to portend a significant event among the Jews. Once in Jerusalem, they learn about the Bethlehem prophesy and, as divine confirmation, the celestial light actually leads them to Bethlehem.
[199] Genesis 1:26-27.

meet the Messiah in Jerusalem, the place where religion was practiced and preserved.

But when they came to the place where Jesus was, the star that started their journey and the scripture that directed it converged—and they found and worshipped the Savior—the Savior Who is Lord of all the stars in heaven[200] and Subject of all the words in sacred scripture.[201]

And they gave Him, the Christ Child, everything they had—gifts fit for a king—gold and frankincense and myrrh. It was the custom in those days and those countries, that important people who came to see great kings would bring them impressive gifts. And they would receive even greater gifts from the kings in return.

The wise men came to the baby Jesus in the customary way. But what could this helpless Infant, born a King in such humble circumstances, give them that would exceed and overshadow the value of their offerings?

The answer is: grace—the forgiveness of sins—the promise of salvation—reconciliation with God—the hope of glory—and the ability to go, from that moment on, a different way.

※

They had seen a star. They had opened God's word. They had come into the presence of Jesus and worshipped Him. And then they heard from God directly in a dream.

And what did God tell them?

"Go a different way!"

This spiritual journey *started* with their going a different way. It reached its *climax* by their going a different way. And it will be *concluded* the same way—by going a different way home. It is not surprising that anyone who has met the Savior of the world and worshipped Him would go through the rest of life a different way.

---

[200] Psalm 147:4.
[201] Luke 24:44-45.

The whole purpose for the appearance of this King-of-the-Jews-and-everybody-else-too was to enable people throughout the world to go a different way—a way they—we—could not go until we saw His star and opened His Word, which always opens a world of revelation to us.

But more than that, by seeing Jesus and worshipping Him and laying our treasures before Him and hearing what His Spirit would say to our hearts, we are led a different way—a wonderful, powerful, happy, holy, redeemed way home.

As it turned out, the wise men couldn't go back from Bethlehem—from Jesus—the same way they came. It was too dangerous for what God was doing when He sent His Son to Bethlehem—and to earth.

There are always those—like Herod and the high priests he consulted—who do not want the world or anybody in it to go a different way. There are those who will not see the signs God sends—and don't want anybody else to see them. There are those who will not listen to God's Word—and don't want anyone else to hear it either. There are those who will go any way they have to to avoid meeting Jesus—who will go out of their way to keep anyone else from going the different way Jesus leads those who find Him and worship Him.

To avoid those people, wise men and women go with Jesus a different way. And the different way of Jesus—as it turns out—leads those who follow it—always—safely home.

The best GPS?

God's Positioning System. God's Precious Savior.

Isaiah 60:1-3, 19-20 ESV

^{1} Arise, shine, for your light has come,
  and the glory of the LORD has risen upon you.
^{2} For behold, darkness shall cover the earth,
  and thick darkness the peoples;
but the LORD will arise upon you,
  and his glory will be seen upon you.
^{3} And nations shall come to your light,
  and kings to the brightness of your rising.

^{19} The sun shall be no more
  your light by day,
nor for brightness shall the moon
  give you light;
but the LORD will be your everlasting light,
  and your God will be your glory.
^{20} Your sun shall no more go down,
  nor your moon withdraw itself;
for the LORD will be your everlasting light,
  and your days of mourning shall be ended.

Going a Different Way

Matthew 2:1-12 ESV

¹ Now after Jesus was born in Bethlehem of Judea in the days of Herod the king, behold, wise men from the east came to Jerusalem, ² saying, "Where is he who has been born king of the Jews? For we saw his star when it rose and have come to worship him." ³ When Herod the king heard this, he was troubled, and all Jerusalem with him; ⁴ and assembling all the chief priests and scribes of the people, he inquired of them where the Christ was to be born. ⁵ They told him, "In Bethlehem of Judea, for so it is written by the prophet:

> ⁶ 'And you, O Bethlehem, in the land of Judah,
>   are by no means least among the rulers of Judah;
>   for from you shall come a ruler
>   who will shepherd my people Israel.'"

⁷ Then Herod summoned the wise men secretly and ascertained from them what time the star had appeared. ⁸ And he sent them to Bethlehem, saying, "Go and search diligently for the child, and when you have found him, bring me word, that I too may come and worship him." ⁹ After listening to the king, they went on their way. And behold, the star that they had seen when it rose went before them until it came to rest over the place where the child was. ¹⁰ When they saw the star, they rejoiced exceedingly with great joy. ¹¹ And going into the house, they saw the child with Mary his mother, and they fell down and worshiped him. Then, opening their treasures, they offered him gifts, gold and frankincense and myrrh. ¹² And being warned in a dream not to return to Herod, they departed to their own country by another way.

36.

Journey's End

Isaiah 60:1-3, 19-20; Matthew 2:1-12 ESV

The Bible tells a story with many journeys. Adam and Eve journey out of Eden because of their sin.[202] Noah and his animals take an ark ride to Mount Ararat for the same reason.[203] Abraham comes from the Chaldean plains into Canaan[204] and his grandson's family goes out of Canaan into Egypt.[205] Centuries later, Moses will lead this greatly enlarged family out of bondage in Egypt[206] and back to Canaan, though the journey for Moses will end at the doorstep of their destination.[207]

David, in his day, will journey from the shepherds' fields of Bethlehem through the caves and hills and battlefields of Judah to a royal throne in Jerusalem.[208] His descendants and their followers will be driven from palace and power into Exile.[209] And a lifetime later, some of their children will come back, singing for joy as they

---

[202] Genesis 3.
[203] Genesis 6—9.
[204] Genesis 12.
[205] Genesis 46.
[206] Exodus 3—15.
[207] Deuteronomy 34.
[208] 1 Samuel 16—2 Samuel 2.
[209] Lamentations 1.

Journey's End

journey to a place they have never been, but know to be their true and rightful home.[210]

In recent weeks, we have watched while Mary and Joseph journeyed from Nazareth in the north to Bethlehem in the south to get a better deal on their taxes,[211] and how Jesus came from heaven to earth on a journey that would lead Him—and all who followed Him—back to heaven in triumph.[212]

Now we read of a group of mysterious men on an even more mysterious journey, guided by perhaps the earliest GPS system on record, going they know not where, to find Someone they've never seen before.

Everyone, it seems, is on a journey.

The wise men journeyed to find Someone. They knew what they were looking for, but not Whom. They knew where to look, but not really. They had a star to follow, but unlike most men, they were also willing to stop and ask directions.

Theirs was a journey of discovery. Though they were foreigners to the faith of Israel, they had enough clues in their own lives to believe there was a journey worth taking to the land of the Jews. Like most pilgrims, they headed for Jerusalem first. Few people headed for Bethlehem—despite what the scripture said. Bethlehem only became a place to go when the world found out what—or Whom—the wise men found there.

The search of the magi came to an end when they came to where Jesus was. Their Christmas quest came to an end when they bestowed their special gifts and bowed down to worship a Child Who, for all their adoration, gave no indication of being anybody special.

But they knew there was more to what they found in Bethlehem than what they saw.

---

[210] Isaiah 40.
[211] Luke 2:1-5.
[212] Ephesians 4:8.

Let's review: these mystery men set out on a journey because they suspected something based on their own experience and exploration. They sought out the Subject of their suspicions.

They followed the light available to them. They received and responded to the revelation of scripture. They put their treasures at the disposal of the Subject of their search, once they found Him. And they became the model for serious seekers and faithful followers for ever after. As a quest, theirs was an unqualified success.

❧

Like them, you and I have come to Bethlehem and found the Child Who was born there.

We, too, were guided by a heavenly light and by holy scripture. We, too, have worshipped the One Who "was born a Child and yet a King."[213] Shall we take a little time, today, at the end of this year, to review our journey thus far?

"Journey," of course, is a metaphor for life. Since ancient times—biblical times—life has been understood as a journey. Because we live, each of us is on a journey. And because of the nature of human life, it is a journey that will one day come to an end for all of us.

You are on a journey, but it is a journey that you were well along on before you realized it—before you woke up one day—from sleep or work or some child's play—and blinked to discover: "My life's a journey!"

And then or later it came to you as well that you've been heading in a direction not of your own choosing—not consciously, anyway—and the momentum of life is just carrying you along, and will continue to carry you—if you don't hit too many bumps in the road you're traveling— a road probably more traveled rather than less.

---

[213] From the hymn, "We Three Kings of Orient Are," John Henry Hopkins, Jr., 1857.

But the more you wake up to the journey you're on, the more concern you will likely feel about the road you're taking—the more you will wonder if the road you're on is the right road to be on.

"Is this the right road? Where does the road I'm on go? Will it take me where I want to go—or where I *should* want to go? And how do I know?

"Is there a road map or a guide? Can I change course if I'm not on the right road? If I can, how and where do I do it?"

When you see your life as a journey, some important questions come to mind.

❧

As I said earlier, each of us is on a journey. But we do not journey alone. We all journey along—in life—together, even if we try to seal ourselves off from others, like riding along in our cars with the windows rolled up. But even then, there are other cars on the road—on every road we travel—and there are other people in those other cars that share the roads we travel.

Other people walk the streets we walk. We see their faces, even if we do not know them. We see their faces, if only for an instant, as they go on down the road of their own journeys. Some of them will walk in step with you—they're "going your way"—and their faces and lives become an ongoing part of your journey, helping or hindering, according to their abilities or their "bent." They make your journey something of what it is—but not all, because it is always *your* journey, and your journey is always about where you've come from and where you're going—and why.

You and I are not merely passersby on our journeys. We are not just coincidental companions going by happenstance in the same direction for a while. We here have chosen to share this journey together. We journey together with a common goal. We share the same destination.

As we journey together, we are grateful for the congenial company. We value the mutual support we have been able to

Epiphany

provide one another, making the journey easier by sharing our meager resources and our abundant concern for each other. And as we look together down the road, we clarify our common vision and strengthen our common resolve to continue on this journey with each other until we reach that place we set out for.

Some have left us along the way to travel different roads, and we wish them well. Others have joined us, seeing the value of this way, and we rejoice in their fellowship on the journey. A few have not so much left us as gone on ahead, reaching the destination before us and waiting to welcome us when we arrive. We cherish them and celebrate their journey's end.

All of us will complete this journey, whether soon or late. But not all will arrive at the same place. Not all will know the joy and satisfaction that waits at the end of the route we have chosen to take on our journey.

On this route we have chosen for our journey, we also, like the magi, have a light to guide us. The world is dark around us, but we journey in a great and steady light. As with the wise men, our light brings us to Jesus because that is where the light has been sent to lead us.

The light we have seen and now follow is not the focusing of our own will or wisdom. Nor is it the collective will of our wayward world. It, like everything else in our experience that is good and pure and true, is the creation and gift of a gracious and all-powerful God Who knows where we were always meant to be—the only place where our journeys and our lives will be complete.

The point of our journeys—yours and mine and everyone's—is to go home. And our only true and permanent home is with the Father Who has prepared a home for us.[214]

It is no easy journey; it is a hard way home for all of us. How often have we sung and not realized we were singing about this journey…

---

[214] John 14:2.

Journey's End

> "Through many dangers, toils and snares,
> I have already come.
> Tis grace hath brought me safe this far,
> and grace...will lead me...home."?[215]

For the wise men, the quest ended in Bethlehem—but not the journey. They still had to go home. But having found Jesus, and having worshipped Him, they *could* go home—and did so—though they went another way.

Bethlehem is not our home; it is not our journey's end. Our journey ends with God our Father, for our home is in heaven with Him. Bethlehem is not our home, but it is the place we must pass through to get home.

Our home is with God our Father, but a Child shall lead us on our journey there—on our journey home—a Child born in Bethlehem—a Child Who was also God—God at His birth and forever before that—God when He grew up and died on the Cross and rose from the dead and reigns as God forever more.

Everybody is on a journey. Life is a journey. Like our spiritual ancestors, we may go on our journey, singing for joy, because though we are going to a place we have never been before—though the way is hard and may be long—our journey will end at home—our true and rightful home—with God. For the Lord will lead us—*is* leading us—together—all the way—all the way home—to Him.

---

[215] From the hymn, "Amazing Grace," John Newton, 1779.

Indices

Sermon Titles in Alphabetical Order

Title	Page
And Along Come John	53
Born Today	183
Born that Men No More May Die	207
Christmas Almost Didn't Happen	109
Come Closer	169
Come Down, Lord!	13
God Like Us	199
God's Advance Man	59
God's Joy	81
Going a Different Way	239
Here He Comes	41
Impossible Child	119
In the Flesh	195
Is Jesus the One?	67
Journey's End	247
Looking for Jesus—Finding the Christ	227
Magnify and Rejoice	135
O Come, Let God Adore Us!	89
Patient Salvation	47
Restore Our Fortunes	73

Sermon Titles in Alphabetical Order

Title **Page**

The Christmas Problem 95
The Christmas Story 153
The Christmas Story (Abridged) 159
The Days Are Coming 29
The Lord is With You 115
The Most Natural Thing in the World 177
The Next Time He Comes… 21
The One of Peace 127
The Time Came 163

Understanding the Time 5
Unto Us a Son is Given 189

What Are You Waiting For? 29
What Did You Get for Christmas? 215
What's Got into That Boy? 223
Where Are You Going for Christmas? 145

Your Part in the Process 103

Sermon Texts in Biblical Order

Text	Title	Page
Genesis		
17:15-19	Impossible Child	118
Psalm		
126	Restore Our Fortunes	73
Isaiah		
9:2, 6-7	Unto Us a Son is Given	188
11:1-10	Your Part in the Process	101
	Christmas Almost Didn't Happen	101
52:7-10	Going a Different Way	237
60:1-3, 19-20	Journey's End	245
63:15-19	Come Down, Lord!	11
64:1-9	Come Down, Lord!	11
Jeremiah		
33:14-16	What Are You Waiting For?	27
33:14-16	The Days Are Coming…	35
Micah		
5:2-5a	The One of Peace	125
Zephaniah		
3:14-20	God's Joy	79
3:14-20	O Come, Let God Adore Us	88
Malachi		
3:1-3	And Along Came John	50
4:5-6	And Along Came John	50

Sermon Texts in Biblical Order

Text	Title	Page
Matthew		
1:18-25	The Christmas Problem	94
1:18-25	Your Part in the Process	102
	Christmas Almost Didn't Happen	102
2:1-12	Going a Different Way	238
	Journey's End	246
3:1-3	Here He Comes	41
11:2-11	Is Jesus the One?	66
Mark		
13:24-37	The Next Time He Comes	19
Luke		
1:5-25	And Along Came John	51
1:26-35	Impossible Child	118
1:26-38	The Lord is With You	114
1:46b-55	Magnify and Rejoice	133
2:1-20	Where Are You Going for Christmas?	142
	The Christmas Story	142
	The Christmas Story (Abridged)	142
	The Time Came	142
	Come Closer	142
	The Most Natural Thing in the World	142
	Born Today	142
	Unto Us a Son is Given	142
2:41-52	What's Got into That Boy?	221
	Looking for Jesus—Finding the Christ	221
3:1-6	God's Advance Man	58
21:25-36	What Are You Waiting For?	28

Sermon Texts in Biblical Order

Text	Title	Page
John		
1:1-14	In the Flesh	195
1:1-5, 9-14	God Like Us	199
Romans		
13:11-14	Understanding the Time	5
Galatians		
4:4-7	What Did You Get for Christmas?	215
Philippians		
4:4-7	God's Joy	80
Hebrews		
2:10-18	Born that Men No More May Die	206
2 Peter		
3:8-15b	Patient Salvation	45

Sermon Texts in Lectionary Order

Date	Text	Page
Cycle A		
Advent 1	Romans 13:11-14	5
Advent 2	Isaiah 11:1-10	101
	Matthew 3:1-3	41
Advent 3	Matthew 11:2-11	66
	Luke 1:46b-55	133
Advent 4	Matthew 1:18-25	94, 102
Christmas 1	Hebrews 2:10-18	206
Epiphany 3	Isaiah 9:2, 6-7	188
Proper 18 [23]	Romans 13:11-14	5
Proper 23 [28]	Philippians 4:4-7	80
Cycle B		
Advent 1	Isaiah 64:1-9	11
	Mark 13:24-37	19
	Luke 1:46b-55	133
Advent 2	2 Peter 3:8-15b	45
Advent 3	Psalm 126	73
	John 1:1-14	195
Advent 4	Luke 1:26-35	118
	Luke 1:26-38	114
	Luke 1:46b-55	133
Christmas 1	Galatians 4:4-7	215

Sermon Texts in Lectionary Order

Date	Text	Page

Cycle B (continued)

Lent 2	Genesis 17:15-19	118
Proper 25 [30]	Psalm 126	73
Thanksgiving	Psalm 126	73

Cycle C

Advent 1	Jeremiah 33:14-16	27, 35
	Luke 21:25-36	28
Advent 2	Malachi 3:1-3	50
	Luke 3:1-6	58
Advent 3	Zephaniah 3:14-20	79, 88
	Philippians 4:4-7	80
Advent 4	Micah 5:2-5a	125
	Luke 1:46b-55	133
Christmas 1	Luke 2:41-52	221
Lent 5	Psalm 126	73
Thanksgiving	Philippians 4:4-7	80

Sermon Texts in Lectionary Order

Date	Text	Page
Cycle ABC		
Christmas	John 1:1-14	195
	John 1:1-5, 9-14	199
Christmas Day 1	Isaiah 9:2, 6-7	188
	Luke 2:1-20	142
Christmas Day 2	Luke 2:1-20	142
Christmas Day 3	Isaiah 52:7-10	237
	John 1:1-14	195
	John 1:1-5, 9-14	199
Holy Name	Galatians 4:4-7	215
Epiphany	Isaiah 60:1-3, 19-20	245
	Matthew 2:1-12	238, 246
Presentation	Malachi 3:1-3	50
	Hebrews 2:10-18	206
Annunciation	Luke 1:26-35	118
	Luke 1:26-38	114
Easter Vigil	Zephaniah 3:14-20	79, 88

Additional Scriptures Referenced

Text	Title	Page
Genesis		
1	Come Down, Lord!	14
1	Patient Salvation	48
1—2	And Along Came John	53
1:3	God Like Us	200
1:26-27	Impossible Child	120
1:26-27	Going a Different Way	242
1:26-28	God Like Us	202
1:28	The Most Natural Thing in the World	180
2:15-17	Born that Men No More May Die	210
3	Unto Us a Son is Given	190
3	Journey's End	247
4—5	Unto Us a Son is Given	190
6—9	Journey's End	247
11	God Like Us	202
12	Journey's End	247
12—21	And Along Came John	53
12—25	Unto Us a Son is Given	190
21:1-7	Impossible Child	120
25—33	Unto Us a Son is Given	190
28:16	Where Are You Going for Christmas?	146
28:16	God Like Us	200
37—50	Unto Us a Son is Given	191
37:5-11	Your Part in the Process	104
46	Journey's End	247
50:20	Your Part in the Process	104
Exodus		
3—15	Journey's End	247
3—15	And Along Came John	53
13:17-22	Come Down, Lord!	14
14	Come Down, Lord!	14

Additional Scriptures Referenced

Text	Title	Page
Exodus (Continued)		
19:1-6	Come Down, Lord!	14
20:1-17	Come Down, Lord!	14
25:8	God Like Us	201
29:45	God Like Us	201
Deuteronomy		
34	Journey's End	147
Joshua		
6	Come Down, Lord!	14
1 Samuel		
1	And Along Came John	53
1:19-20	Impossible Child	122
2:2	God Like Us	201
16	And Along Came John	53
16	Unto Us a Son is Given	191
16—22	Journey's End	247
17	Come Down, Lord!	15
2 Samuel		
1—2	Journey's End	247
5	Unto Us a Son is Given	191
7:1-17	The Days Are Coming…	37
11—12	Unto Us a Son is Given	191
1 Kings		
1—2, 10	Unto Us a Son is Given	191
17—22	And Along Came John	54
18:20-40	Come Down, Lord!	15

Additional Scriptures Referenced

Text	Title	Page
2 Kings		
1—2	And Along Came John	54
Job		
1:21	Born that Men No More May Die	209
39:26-27	God Like Us	201
40:4	God Like Us	201
Psalms		
24:1	Patient Salvation	48
90:2, 9	God Like Us	201
147:4	Going a Different Way	243
Isaiah		
9:7	The One of Peace	131
40	Journey's End	248
40:4	God's Advance Man	62
53:3	The Next Time He Comes	24
55:6	What's Got into That Boy?	225
55:8	God Like Us	201
Jeremiah		
21:4-6	The Christmas Story	155
29:10	Restore Our Fortunes	75
29:13	What's Got into That Boy?	225
52	Restore Our Fortunes	75
Lamentations		
1	Journey's End	247

Additional Scriptures Referenced

Text	Title	Page
Daniel		
7	And Along Came John	54
7:13	The Next Time He Comes	23
Micah		
5:2-5	Going a Different Way	240
Matthew		
1	Unto Us a Son is Given	191
1—2	God's Joy	85
1:18	In the Flesh	196
1:18-23	God Like Us	200
1:18-25	The Time Came	164
2:1-2, 9-11	Going a Different Way	240
2:1-12	The One of Peace	127
2:1-12	The Time Came	165
2:12	Your Part in the Process	103
2:12	Going a Different Way	240
2:12-13	Born that Men No More May Die	207
2:13-14	Come Closer	173
2:14	Born that Men No More May Die	207
2:14-15	Going a Different Way	240
2:16-17	Born that Men No More May Die	208
2:19-23	Come Closer	173
2:21-23	Going a Different Way	240
3:17	God's Joy	85
4:13	Come Closer	173
6:25, 33	The One of Peace	130
7:7	What's Got Into That Boy?	225
11:5	Unto Us a Son is Given	192
16:13-14	Is Jesus the One?	68

Additional Scriptures Referenced

Text	Title	Page

Matthew (Continued)

26:36	Come Closer	173
28:1-6	What are You Waiting For?	32
28:1-7	The Lord is With You	116
28:20	Looking for Jesus—Finding the Christ	228

Mark

1:16-20	Born Today	185
11:15	Come Closer	173
15:46	Come Closer	173

Luke

1—2	God's Joy	85
1:5-11	Your Part in the Process	103
1:26	In the Flesh	196
1:26-33	Your Part in the Process	103
1:37	Impossible Child	124
1:39-40	Going a Different Way	240
1:57-66	Impossible Child	122
1:66-79	Magnify and Rejoice	138
2	Unto Us a Son is Given	191
2:1-5	Journey's End	248
2:4-5	Going a Different Way	240
2:6	Born that Men No More May Die	211
2:8-14	Your Part in the Process	103
2:8-20	What are You Waiting For?	32
2:8-20	Going a Different Way	240
2:14	Magnify and Rejoice	138
2:14	Born that Men No More May Die	207
2:16-20	What's Got Into That Boy?	224
2:22	Come Closer	173
2:22-38	What are You Waiting For?	32

Additional Scriptures Referenced

Text	Title	Page
Luke (Continued)		
2:22-40	Looking for Jesus—Finding the Christ...	229
2:29-32	Magnify and Rejoice..................................	138
3:21-22	What are You Waiting For?.........................	32
3:23	What are You Waiting For?.........................	32
19:10	Looking for Jesus—Finding the Christ...	232
19:45-48	Looking for Jesus—Finding the Christ...	230
23:44-46	What are You Waiting For?.........................	32
24:44-45	Going a Different Way..............................	243
John		
1:1-18	The Time Came...	164
1:12	Impossible Child	123
1:12-13	What Did You Get for Christmas?..........	219
1:14	Impossible Child	123
1:14	The Most Natural Thing in the World....	179
1:29	Born Today	185
1:36-39	Come Closer..	173
3:16	Patient Salvation..	48
14:1-3	The Next Time He Comes…....................	26
14:2	Journey's End...	251
14:15-17	What Did You Get for Christmas?..........	219
14:27	The One of Peace	132
16:21	God's Joy...	85
16:22	God's Joy...	85
16:33	The One of Peace	132
18:1-14	What are You Waiting For?.........................	32
18:37	What's Got into That Boy?.......................	225
19:17	Come Closer..	173
Acts		
9:1-9	Born Today	185

Additional Scriptures Referenced

Text	Title	Page
Romans		
1:18-32	Come Down, Lord	16
3:1-26	God Like Us	202
4:13-21	Impossible Child	121
5:1	The One of Peace	131
5:3-5	What Did You Get for Christmas?	219
5:12, 18	Born that Men No More May Die	210
8:11	Patient Salvation	48
8:31	The Christmas Story	156
8:32	The Christmas Story	156
8:38-39	The One of Peace	130
1 Corinthians		
1:25	God Like Us	201
15:12-19	Patient Salvation	48
15:35-53	The Next Time He Comes	24
15:50	In the Flesh	197
2 Corinthians		
5:19	The Christmas Problem	100
5:19	Where Are You Going for Christmas?	151
5:21	Born that Men No More May Die	210
Ephesians		
4:8	Journey's End	248
Philippians		
2:5-8	God Like Us	204
2:5-8	Born that Men No More May Die	209
2:6-7	The Most Natural Thing in the World	179
2:9-10	The Christmas Problem	99

Additional Scriptures Referenced

Text	Title	Page
Philippians	**(Continued)**	
2:10-11	The Next Time He Comes	23
4:7	The One of Peace	131
Colossians		
3:15	The One of Peace	131
Hebrews		
1:3	Come Closer	173
2:14-15	In the Flesh	198
4:14-15	God Like Us	204
11:11-13	Impossible Child	121
12:2	God's Joy	85
1 John		
3:2	The Next Time He Comes	23
Revelation		
7:14	What are You Waiting For?	33
16:16	What are You Waiting For?	33
19:11-16	The Next Time He Comes	25

www.ingramcontent.com/pod-product-compliance
Lightning Source LLC
Chambersburg PA
CBHW020847090426
42736CB00008B/276